Success is
Waiting for you

Ryan C. Greene

SUCCESS *Is In Your* HAND

19 KEYS TO UNLOCKING THE SUCCESSFUL PERSON YOU WERE DESIGNED TO BE

RYAN C. GREENE
Founder & CEO of Maximum Leadership Concepts

Foreword By **Bishop Jerome Stokes**, Author of *You Can Do It*

Success Is In Your Hand
19 Keys To Unlocking The Successful Person You Were Designed To Be

Copyright © 2004, 2006 Ryan C. Greene
www.ryancgreene.com
www.bakaribooks.com

All Rights Reserved. No part of this publication may be reproduced, stored in a retrieval system, or transmitted in any form by means electronic, mechanical, photocopying, recording or otherwise, except for the inclusion of brief quotations in a review, without prior permission in writing from the publisher.

All Bible verses are taken from the King James Version of the Bible

Cover Design by RCGraphics
Photography by KayBee McClarine

ISBN 978-0-9779034-0-5

Published in Baltimore, MD, by Bakari Book Publishers

Baltimore

*This book is dedicated to my loving wife, Leslie,
who has stuck with me through the good and bad times.
You are my reason why I push so hard and never give up.
Thank you for your temporary sacrifices so that we
may possess permanent increase.*

*To my late mother, Jacqueline M. Kidd.
I wish you could see how all of your hard work turned out.
I love you and I will forever miss you.
See you later.*

Ryan C. Greene

Acknowledgements

With special thanks,

My family for all of your love and support. Thank you for not trying to clip my wings when I was ready to fly.

Hampton University for being a model institution for developing leaders all across the world and setting the pace for what an HBCU really should be. Too bad the whole world can't be one big H.U.

All of my business partners and mentors in Pre-Paid Legal Services, Inc and Team NuVision. Thank you for making dreams become reality. Darnell Self, Antonio Adair and Michael Humes thank you for showing me how to attain the success and lifestyle I've always dreamed of as well as teaching me how to become a great leader.

My pastor, Bishop Jerome Stokes of Church of the Redeemed of the Lord in Baltimore, MD. "What does it profit a man to gain the whole world yet lose his soul?" Thank you for your spiritual leadership and guidance and literally saving my soul. You are the epitome of success. Thank you for validating my book with your foreword. And to my entire CRL family, I love you and God Bless you all.

To my Editor, Latonya Gibson, thanks for all of your hard work and great advice. We have to do this again sometime.

To everyone whom I have ever crossed paths with, whether good or bad, I thank you or making me who I am today. I wish each of you all the success in the world.

Ryan C. Greene

Success Is In Your Hand
Table of Contents

Foreword

Introduction: Success Is In Your Hand   15

Your Success Is Your Decision
Chapter 1: Your Success Is Waiting For You   23

Chapter 2: Develop a Strong WHY   33

Three Keys To Unlocking The Successful You
Chapter 3: Your Attitude   45
    For as a man thinketh in his heart, so is he

Chapter 4: Your Personal Development   57
    Study to show thyself approved

Chapter 5: Your Belief   79
    For we walk by faith not by sight

From Dreams To Reality
Chapter 6: More Keys to Unlocking Your Success   91

Chapter 7: Your Game Plan for Success   119

Conclusion   133

About The Author

Ryan C. Greene

Foreword

It's amazing when you look at the way some people carry out their lives. I'm even amazed, when I look back in retrospect, at the way I have carried out my life at times. That's because in life it is possible to be busily engaged in a lot of activities but going nowhere. We can wear ourselves out and still not get ahead. Perhaps many of us have experienced situations where we have worked hard and with all of our labor and the time we have put in, we are still not getting ahead.

This state could give the feeling of a soldier marking time. I believe we can come to feel as though we are marking time in our lives. We are steadily moving, but moving in place, not actually going anywhere, so we are marking time. It is one thing when a soldier marks time, it's another thing when in our lives we are marking time. Time is one thing we don't want to waste.

There are a lot of people currently stuck in a position in life and they have been stuck for along time. Some do not have the courage to make the necessary adjustments to change their lives, while others lack the drive that is necessary for change. The ironic thing is that many of them do not like where they are, but they allow themselves to stay there because they will not do what is necessary to move from the place that they are in. So, instead of moving ahead, they are very busy maintaining ground and maintaining their posture or position in the very place where they don't want to be.

Most people have some area in their lives in which they want to move forward. For a long time they have been saying they are going to move forward, but they have yet to do so. How long have you told yourself, "I'm going to change this", "I'm moving from this place", "I'm not going to deal with this situation any longer", "I've had enough"? How long have you told yourself that things need to change knowing that you have the power or access to the power to bring that change, but yet, you do not act on it? Telling ourselves and not doing anything leaves us in a position of non-fulfillment and also builds a pocket of unhappiness in our lives. The areas of my life that I know I needed to change but did not, very readily pronounced their presence in my life. They let me know they are there. Every time I think about those areas I am reminded of how much I dislike them. When I look at the fact that I should move and have the ability to move, but I don't, it causes me to feel frustrated with myself.

A lot of people are sitting back waiting for God and God is sitting back waiting for them to do what's necessary. Many of you can do things without divine intervention or involvement of the Lord directly. So because many people don't move and don't do anything, many people stagnate. To stagnate is to be inactive. We can be busy with activity but our lives can be stagnating because although we are doing a lot, we are not really going anywhere. The fact that a person is busy does not mean they are going anywhere. The fact that a person works a job, goes to church, and is involved in organizations is not a sign that they are necessarily moving forward in their lives. It is simply a sign that they are doing what they are doing.

Stagnation occurs in many areas of our lives. It occurs in our family life, our careers, our education, our finances, and our leadership ability. Causes of stagnation can be laziness, low self-esteem, negative influences of others, discouragement, depression, consecutive failures, poor stewardship and lack of ambition. Results of stagnation include lack of progress, lack of increased productivity, it hinders the expansion of the body of Christ, and it hinders personal and spiritual growth.

We have to overcome this and know there is going to come a time when we look at our lives and say, "It's time for me to move", "It's time for me to change", and "It's time for me to do something different". God has given each of us a divine purpose and a mission to accomplish on earth. Stagnation has stopped too many people from fulfilling their destiny and receiving the full reward and blessing that God has for them. The fact that you are reading this book is a warning to the enemy that you are ready, willing and able to break free of his mental grips and free yourself from his chains of mediocrity and walk into your purpose. By the time you complete this book and apply what you have read, success will truly be in your hand. I congratulate you for taking charge of your life and encourage you to possess all that God has promised you.

God Bless You,
Bishop Jerome Stokes
Pastor, Church of the Redeemed of the Lord

Introduction

What is success? What makes someone successful? Why do so many people strive to have it? Why does it seem to elude so many others? How do we know when we have it? Is a millionaire successful? What about a man who has lost it all? Is the winner of an election successful? What about the person they defeated? Does getting a promotion on your job make you successful? How about if you were fired?

Success is a strange phenomenon. It's much like beauty; it's in the eye of the beholder. Others will try to tell you what determines success and whether or not you are successful but only you can truly determine your level of success. Only you know what the plan for your life is and the road you must take to get there. I define success as becoming that which you were called to be through the continual unfolding of God's design and purpose for your life.

Material things or social status should not determine success. Those things may serve as outward indicators of success or be the byproducts of success, but they can also be used as a front to portray a false image of success. Because someone drives a luxury car or lives in a million dollar home does not mean they are successful. They could be a doctor, a business owner, a lottery winner or even a drug dealer. Many times those same people in the big homes are just like 97% of Americans, up to their ears in debt and just a check or two away from losing it all.

The problem most people face is they would rather kill themselves to support a lifestyle they cannot afford than to live within their means. People are too concerned about what others will think of them. You can only fake success for so long before time tells on you. Success is an ongoing process that can best be achieved by overcoming failures not avoiding them. Willie Jolley says it best in the title of his book *A Setback is a Setup for a Comeback*.

Success Is In Your Hand is not designed to tell you "This is success" or "this is not success" but rather it is intended to help you put together the combination to unlock what God has already put in you so that you may excel at what it is He put you here to do. It's up to you to discover your purpose. Ask God to reveal to you why you are here. Once He reveals your purpose, this book will equip you with principles to help you develop a successful mindset and the successful behaviors to carry you along the way. The principles and concepts in this book will be your tools to break free from a mediocre mindset, to stop settling for less than you deserve and to increase your belief that you can achieve the impossible.

Your success lies within you. It's already in your hand so no one can give it to you. It's up to you to decide, "Enough is enough! I am more than a conqueror, and God has promised me the desires of my heart." What would you do, if your life circumstances were different, to make your mark on the world? What dream keeps you up every night but you've told yourself it was too big for you? If you did not have to go to work in the morning what would you do with all of that time? Whose life would you change? How successful would you become?

COUNT IT ALL JOY

James 1:2 says to "Count it all joy" and sometimes that is difficult to do. It's hard to see the blessing in every situation and circumstance especially when God puts you through something rough in order to bless someone else. In September 2003 my good friend and business partner, Allan Gray, took his wife and two kids to Disney World. It was their first family vacation in years. About halfway through the vacation Allan calls me and asks me if I could drive by his home and check on things because someone called him from his wife's cell phone but his wife was obviously in Florida with him. I agreed to drive by the house only to find that their home had been broken into. It was one of the highest forms of violation and I felt like it was my own home that had been broken into.

I agreed to stay there and wait for the police and take care of things while they "enjoyed" the rest of their vacation. That evening Allan's mother and Mr. Brooks ("Mr. B") came over as well. We sat in that house waiting for the police to come and investigate for about six to seven hours. In that time we had plenty of time to talk. Mr. B is a businessman who has made and even lost millions of dollars so as a businessman myself it was an honor to have the time to pick his brain. I shared with him my business dreams and goals and some of the obstacles I had encountered. He very quickly suggested that I read *The One Minute Millionaire* by Mark Victor Hansen and Robert G. Allen. I'm thinking if a businessman of his caliber says this book is going to help me then I have got to get that book.

I searched all the libraries for over a month and a half before I could finally find the book. I'm not going to tell you what the book was about but I will tell you that the book flat out changed my life. The practical easy to apply information gave me the belief that I could achieve all that I was pursuing. It made me see that instead of wasting time talking about my dream I could be using time building and living my dream. After reading that book I began to put the pieces together and do what I had been dreaming about for so long. The book showed me that money is simply an inanimate object with so many ways to create it that the lack of it cannot really be used as an excuse to not go after your dreams. Money is like Kool-Aid, when you make it it doesn't last long and when it's gone you've got to make some more. That book played a major role in why I even wrote this book. *After* you read this book I encourage you to read *The One Minute Millionaire*.

Let me bring it home. I had been praying to God for the answer and a plan for the way out of my wilderness but like most humans do so often, I was trying to work *my* plan while I was waiting for God to "come up" with His. Little did I know that God in His perfect timing was answering my prayer through the tragedy of someone else. You see I would have never read the *One Minute Millionaire* had Mr. B not told me to. Mr. B would have never told me to read it if we had not spent those six to seven hours together. We would have never spent those six to seven hours together if the police had not taken all night to get to the house to investigate. We would have never been there if Allan and his family did not go on vacation. And if they did not go on vacation then their house would have never been broken into.

Now I'm not happy that my friend's home was broken into but what if we got there and complained all night. What if the police would have gotten there in only two hours? That conversation would have never happened and I might still be trying to figure out the direction I should go in life. Only God could have orchestrated an answer to a prayer so perfectly and only an open mind to hear His word could have received it. A lot of us have the answer to our prayers right in front of us but because that's not what we prayed for we leave our blessings on the table and forfeit our success.

Since that day in September Mr. B and I have not spent so much as five minutes talking. If I did not take heed to what he said when he said it then that opportunity could have been lost forever. When God answers your prayer it is up to you to jump on it. He's not going to beg you. When it comes to seizing the day and acting on your dream there is no tomorrow. How many blessings have you procrastinated on and forgot all about because the opportunity passed? It may not look the way you expected it would but if God sent it then I assure you it couldn't be any more perfect.

Allan and his family were blessed throughout the ordeal as well. Within a week the police caught the burglars and they recovered their belongings and God continues to bless Allan's family 30, 60 and 100 fold. The point of all of this is to count it all joy. Your tragedies and hard times could be building blocks for you or they could be someone else's doorway to their blessing.

Success Is In Your Hand will teach you why a positive attitude, constant personal development and strong belief in yourself and in God are key to unlocking the successful you. If I hadn't kept a positive attitude in the bad situation I was in then I would have overlooked the positives before me. If I were not open to personal development then I would have never read the book recommended to me. If I did not believe in myself then I would have never acted on my dreams and if I did not believe God ordained my success then I would have quit when things got too tough. I only make one guarantee to anyone reading this book; once you read it and apply the principles to your life your mind will be transformed and you will unlock the successful person you were designed to be.

Ryan C. Greene

YOUR SUCCESS IS WAITING FOR YOU
Believe and act as though it were impossible to fail

"Success is not determined by the final destination but by the road you take to get there"
-Ryan C. Greene, Author

"He shall be like a tree planted by the rivers of water, that bringeth forth his fruit in his season; his leaf also shall not wither; and whatsoever he doeth shall prosper"
-Psalms 1:3, Holy Bible

Let me start right out by saying, this book is not for everybody. This book is only for those who are sick and tired of being sick and tired of their life circumstances. This book is for those people who know God has purposed them for something bigger in their life but they are stuck in mediocrity. This book is designed for people who are striving to reach higher levels of success regardless of their current position in life. This book is for those who are looking to unlock the successful person God designed them to be.

> Success is waiting for you

If you are any one of the people I described, then this is what you have been looking for. Success is waiting for you. It is your time to unlock your success and walk in your divine destiny and purpose. Today can be the first day of the rest of your successful life if that is what you truly desire. God has already predestined your life, but it is up to you to walk the path He has laid for you.

I don't believe in coincidence or good luck, I believe in one true and living God who orchestrates the entire universe. The B.I.B.L.E. (Basic Instructions Before Leaving Earth) serves as an instruction manual for every aspect of our life. God reveals to us in His Word how to live our lives, conduct our business and all the promises He has waiting for those who abide in His Word. I believe God has something special in store for each person that reads this book and applies its principles to their life. The key is the application of the material. Many people read Self-Help books but they never do what the book teaches. Unlocking your success is going to take hard work, sacrifice, dedication and desire. But you don't have to take my word for it. Here are just a few of the ways that success has been summarized:

"Success is internal. Others try to judge your success by what they see but true success comes from within."

"Success is the continual unfolding of the design and purpose of your life."

"Real success is finishing your cause."

"Success is not determined by your final destination but by the road you take to get there."

"The essence of your manhood is your legacy. Once you're gone all that matters is the impact that you left with others."

"To be successful, find a way to serve as many people as possible."

"Success is attached to a struggle or process."

"Success is something you attract by the person you become."

"The key to success is life-long learning."

"We are what we repeatedly do, success then is not an act, it is a habit."

I could go on and on with the ways other people define success; however, the most meaningful definition is going to be the one you create. You have to define success for yourself as it pertains to your goals and aspirations for your life. That brings me to the Three Traps you must avoid when trying to unlock your success.

Trap #1: Trying to live out someone else's dream for your life. With everything you do, ask yourself are you doing it because you were called to do it or because you were told to do it. So many people are unsuccessfully trying to achieve things that they were not called to do and they see themselves as failures or not as good as everyone else. The reality is that they were never supposed to be doing that thing in the first place. It is very difficult to be great at something that you are not fully equipped to do. Some people may even experience certain levels of success in areas where they were not called, however, they will never experience abundant success until they are fulfilling their called purpose.

Trap #2: Measuring yourself against the success of other people. Be sure not to measure your success by comparing yourself with other people but by comparing yourself to the vision and purpose God gave YOU. I see it all the time where outsiders pit people against one another as benchmarks for success. You see competition in business, church, sports, and entertainment to name a few. You especially see it among women. Over the last three decades, the music industry has notoriously pitted two women against each other for "Diva of the Decade". In the 2000's there is Britney Spears and Christina Aguillera. The 1990's saw Whitney Houston versus Mariah Carey. And the 1980's had Prince and Michael Jackson. OK maybe the 1980's were questionable, but you get the point. The moment you get caught up measuring your success against someone else's, the more difficult it will be for you to attain success. Don't lose focus of your purpose by being overly concerned with who is better than you.

Trap #3: The fear of losing. This includes the fear of losing material possessions, losing people, losing status, losing money or losing your comfort zone. What people fail to realize is that having material possessions, achieving milestones or gaining recognition is not what makes someone successful. It's the struggles and obstacles that were overcome to obtain those things that make the person successful. Anyone can be successful if they don't have to go through anything to get it, but Psalm 126:5 says, *"They that sow in tears shall reap in joy"*. Be not discouraged by the things you lose for it only makes space for you to gain even more.

The foundational scripture for this book, Matthew 10:29-31, speaks to this point. *So Jesus answered and said, "Assuredly, I say unto you, there is no one who has left house or brothers or sisters or father or mother or wife or children or lands, for My sake and the gospel's, who shall not receive a hundred fold now in this time-houses and brothers and sisters and mothers and children and lands, with persecutions-and in the age to come, eternal life. But many who are first shall be last, and the last shall be first."* –Matthew 10:29-31 KJV

God says that no one who is walking in his purpose will lose anything and not receive one hundred times that which he lost. Even more importantly, He says you will receive your hundred fold blessing *"Now in this time."* You may have to give up some things on your road to success but God promises to reward you in this time while you are still here. Another point that God warns of is that you will receive your success *"with persecutions."* People will talk badly about you when your car gets repossessed and they are going to talk badly about you when you have five cars in your driveway. People will talk badly about you when you are wearing the same suit every week and they are going to talk badly about you when you have a different custom-made suit each day. People will talk badly about you when you cannot find a job and they are going to talk badly about you when you own a multi-million dollar business. Get ready for the persecutions because it is just part of God's promise. Don't be concerned with what others have to say. Always remember, if someone

> *The last shall be first and*
> *The first shall be last*

does not have what you want, and they are not striving to get it, then their opinion doesn't matter.

And finally, in one of the most well known Bible verses, God says, *"the last shall be first and the first shall be last"*. God is telling all those who endure the suffering and persecutions that, when it's all said and done, you will go from last to first. Right now you may feel like life has dealt you a raw deal and instead of sitting on top of the world, the world is sitting on top of you. Everyone around you seems to have all the things you want and you just keep losing more and more ground. But all your hard work and perseverance will pay off in the end. Those same people that persecute you and call you crazy, will be coming to you for help in the end. You will become the lender and not the borrower. You will no longer be weak but strong.

Successful people do now what unsuccessful people are not willing to do so they can have later what unsuccessful people will never have.

MY STORY

I began college at Hampton University in the Fall of 1993. I knew when I graduated from high school that my goal was to become a business owner. Like most freshman I struggled with selecting the right major that would help me fulfill my dreams. I remember my father constantly telling me to major in Economics. I had no idea what Economics was but it sounded to me like it dealt with money so I figured that was the way to go. It wasn't until my second semester that I realized I was living someone else's dream. I did some research and found that everything I felt I needed to know about running a business (Advertising, Retail and Marketing Management, Operations and Sales Management etc,) was covered in the Marketing curriculum and an Economics Degree was not going to get me where I wanted to go. I decided to change my major to Marketing. I enjoyed school a great deal more and my degree has served me well since then. To this day, other than supply and demand, I have never even thought about economics.

As a child, many people told me what I was going to be when I grew up. If I had listened to what other people told me to do with my life I would probably be a preacher right now. My father is a Pastor. Growing up, everyone naturally assumes the preacher's son is going to be a preacher too. I thank God I did not fall into that trap. I may have even been a good preacher but I would have been doing what I was told to do and not what I was called to do. I later found my calling was to involve speaking to groups of people but in a different manner. Today I am a Motivational Speaker and Trainer and the CEO of my own company. While the foundation of all my teachings is based on Godly principles, it is quite different than preaching.

Another trap I had to overcome is the fear of losing. It took a long time for me to come to grips with the theory of short-term pain for long-term permanent gain. I had to realize that sometimes it is necessary to take one step backwards in order to take two giant leaps forward. Becoming successful takes great sacrifice and with sacrifice comes pain. I went back to Matthew 10:29-31 and decided that God's promises far outweighed the promises of man. If I wanted a bigger house then I had to be willing to let go of the smaller one. If I wanted more prosperity, then I had to be willing to experience being dead broke. If I wanted to impact the lives of millions of people then I had to experience being alone in the wilderness. It is the pain that makes the pleasure so wonderful. If you have not experienced the gain you are striving for then perhaps you have not experienced enough pain.

I had to learn to avoid the three traps that prevent people from reaching success. *Trap #1: Trying to live out someone else's dream for your life.* Your greatest success will come from doing what you were purposed and designed to do. Many people will offer their two cents on how you should live your life and it is your choice to either accept their deposit or return it for insufficient funds. *Trap #2: Measuring yourself against the success of others.* When you are operating in your calling, no one will be able to compare to you. Just as when you are operating in someone else's calling, you won't be able to measure up to them. You don't know the story behind someone else's success so be careful what you ask for. *Trap #3: Fear of losing.* When I could truly say that I was willing to give up everything in order to have what God promised me, that is when doors began to open and opportunities began chasing me. I know what God has called me to do. I know what my purpose is. I know that no weapon formed against me shall prosper because I am walking in my purpose.

Your success is waiting for you. Avoiding the traps that snare most people is Step One. Now let's get into the 19 keys to unlocking the successful you.

DEVELOP A STRONG WHY
*Your reason why you want success will determine
If you ever have success or not*

"If a man has not found something worth dying for,
then he is not fit to live"
-Dr. Martin Luther King Jr., Civil Rights Leader

"For God so loved the world, that He gave His only
begotten Son, that whosoever believeth in Him
should not perish, but have everlasting life"
-John 3:16, Holy Bible

Having success is great but you must develop a reason why you want success. That's what this chapter is about. This first key to unlocking the successful you is perhaps the most important and vital key. That key is having a strong Why. Knowing why you strive toward any goal is more crucial than the goal itself. A Why is your driving force. It makes you get out of bed early on a rainy morning to work toward your goal. It keeps you up late at night when you're exhausted and feel like you cannot do anymore. It is what makes you do the impossible and achieve the unbelievable. Just like a soldier on a war mission, your Why is your mission statement for your existence so don't take it lightly.

Too often people start a mission with a goal in mind when in actuality in order to maximize your success potential you need to start with why you even want the goal accomplished. Be careful not to confuse your Why with your goals. Your goal may be to be a millionaire but why you want to be a millionaire will determine whether or not you ever become one (even before you ever take the first step toward it). Take a minute to think about your Why. Why are you willing to go through whatever it takes to achieve your goals? Why can't you stop pursuing your dream even after you've failed time and time again?

> *Be careful not to confuse your Why with your goals*

Your Why is your engine that gives you power to go, your goal is the end destination you seek and your strategy is the roadmap you take to get there. Everything else, the books, seminars, associations etc, will be what tunes you up to get to where you are going as quickly as possible.

Getting to the end is what we all seek but without an engine we're in for a long trip. This chapter is not intended to tell you your Why. I can't do that. You have to determine that for yourself. What I can help you with is how to determine your Why for yourself. My life changed for the better once I figured out exactly why I existed and why I was pursuing my dreams, consequently, I am assured that once you develop a strong enough Why you will be well on your way up the ladder to success.

There are four questions that you should explore and answer to develop your Why.

1. *What motivates you?*

Is it your family? Is it your career? Do you like helping other people? Do you like to be recognized for what you do? Do you want to be rich? Do you need more time in your life? Do you like to travel? Do you have kids? Do you want kids? Are you married? Do you have a ministry within you? Do you like to play instruments? Do you sing or dance or write?

What do you do well that you can't do as much as you'd like to because of your current life situation?

These questions should be enough to get the juices boiling in the right direction. Answer these questions honestly and use the answers as your starting point toward your Why. If you are going to spend any part of your life pursuing anything worthwhile then you have to want to do it and you have to enjoy the journey. Finding out what motivates you will keep you pushing through the storm even when you have no umbrella.

The majority of workers in America are dissatisfied with their current jobs. They feel exploited, under appreciated and disenfranchised; however, they continue to sacrifice their time, their life and their dreams for something they passionately hate. They have no motivation to go above and beyond at work because the return is too often not worth the sacrifice to get it. However, the more motivated and fulfilled you are by something the more you are willing to go through to achieve it. When developing your Why, take serious consideration about what motivates you to action. A Why is not worth the paper it's written on if it's not going to push you toward achieving your goals.

2. Who or what is at the center of your Why?

Most unsuccessful people find themselves constantly struggling to reach higher levels in life because their reason why only revolves around themselves. Everything they do begins with the question, "What's in it for me?" They want success because they want to buy things or gain recognition or even appear above others. On the contrary, most successful people have Whys that are centered on someone or some cause other than themselves. Their blessings come because of a desire to make an impact on someone else's life. They've learned to place the needs of others before their own.

Think about it, we have a much easier time letting ourselves down than letting others down. We let ourselves down all the time

> *"Most successful people have whys that are centered on someone or some cause other than themselves"*

and just keep on going on with life. How many times have you said, "I'm going to lose weight", "I'm going to go back to school and get a degree" or even "I'm going to start my own business" but you never did it. It was easy to let yourself down. What if you would have said, "I'm going to lose weight so I can live a long life and be around for my family", "I'm going back to school in order to have more to offer to those that count on me" or "I'm starting my own business so that my grandchildren will never have to work and run from bill collectors". Notice the difference? When you do things for others it becomes more difficult to quit when things get rough.

You don't want your great grandchildren to see your picture in the family photo album 50 years from now and ask, "Who is this" and their parents say, "That's your great granddad. He really let us down. He always said he was going to start a business but he always said tomorrow. He always said he would sacrifice today so that we would not have to work but he listened to his negative friends and gave up on his dreams. Here's your great grandmother, she always quit when things got rough and let her fear take over instead of fighting through her troubles. She always said God would provide all her needs and she could do all things through Him but I guess she never really believed it."

That's a sad situation but the reality is that it happens everyday. When your Why is centered on the right people or cause it will drive you harder and push you through the pain more than if it were just about you.

3. Is it strong enough to make you cry?

Your Why can't be weak. "I want to be rich" is not strong enough. Ninety-seven percent of people will never be rich so to want to be rich is more than likely not motivation enough to keep you going through the hard times you will face trying to become rich. You need to evaluate the reason why you want to be rich and focus on that. Your Why has to be so strong that if you quit before you're done it will make you cry. My mentor and friend Michael Humes told me this some time ago and I had to revamp my whole reasoning. This is why, as I stated earlier, most successful people's Why is not even about them. It almost always is centered on making life better for someone else.

How much longer are you going to settle for being average simply because it's easier than working hard to achieve excellence? How long are you going to be afraid to answer your phone because you know it's a bill collector? How long will you wonder whether or not your car will still be outside each morning? How long will you prostitute your skills and abilities to a job you hate just to get a check instead of building something for yourself? How long are you going to live outside of God's will for your life yet expect Him to fix everything for you?

Take an honest inventory of your current life situation and ask yourself if you like what you see. How do you feel about where you are in life? Have you reached the levels of success you thought you would by this time? The sad reality is most people are not happy. Instead of getting depressed about where you currently are use that to push you toward where you can be. When you realize there is a way out and you don't want to be where you are then quitting will never be an option. If the thought of you quitting does not bring tears to your eyes because of how it is going to affect you and those depending on you, then your Why is not strong enough.

4. Is it worth dying for?

Dr. Martin Luther King Jr. said, "If a man has not found something worth dying for, then he is not fit to live". His Why was to have equality for all races and it was, to him, a Why that was worth dying. Think about all the opposition that Dr. King fought against to achieve his Why: the hatred, the police arrests and brutality, the house and church bombings, the constant stress on he and his family and ultimately his life. All for people that he did not even know. So what's stopping you? Are your obstacles really that big? Had Dr. Kings Why only been about him, his name probably would have never been mentioned in the history books because he would have quit long before the first news story could have ever been written. But even at the age of 26 he understood the power of having a cause worth dying for and it motivated him to change the way an entire country was governed. It is because of the Why he possessed almost

> *If a man has not found something worth dying for, then he is not fit to live*

50 years ago that I can even write this book today and anyone who desires to read it can read it. Don't take your Why lightly; someone else 50 years from now will be counting on you to make his or her life better.

Asking yourself is something worth dying for does not mean you are asking death to knock on your door or that you are actually going to die because of it; however, it does state that death is the only thing that will stop you from pursuing your Why. That's a huge advantage over others that don't have that. When your back is against the wall and there seems like there's no way out, as long as you're alive you can keep on fighting. That cannot be taught. Having a strong enough why will give you that attitude automatically.

Paul of the Bible said he died daily to sin so he could live for Christ. What is it that you need to die to so that your life will be better? Why wouldn't you be willing to die for financial freedom when you are already killing yourself simply to live check to check? Instead of spending your time complaining about your life, find someone whom you would go through anything for to make his or her life better. Being willing to die for your Why gives you the resolve to say "I will…Until" and never give up.

If you haven't done so already take a few minutes now to go through these four questions and develop your Why and

WRITE IT DOWN. Use it as your beginning to unlocking the successful you. Once you realize Why you want to be successful it becomes easier to figure out how to become successful.

MY STORY

I went through twelve years of grade school, four years of undergrad and I worked for five years after that and no one ever asked me "Why?" I had plenty of goals and I knew what I wanted to be when I "grew up", but I was never asked why I wanted those things. The sad part was that after investing all that time and effort, I had grown up and still wasn't what I wanted to be and I did not have what I wanted to have but even worse I did not know why. After all, I did like my parents told me; I went to school, got a good education, went on to get a good job but, I still was not happy.

Growing up I always knew that I wanted to be a business owner and make millions of dollars so I could make life easier for my family and friends. The problem was the road I was taking (Strategy) wasn't getting me to my end destination (Goal) because my engine (Why) was stalled. Growing up my Why was like a lot of kids, to make my parents happy; however, when I was old enough I realized that it was more important that I pursue my own dreams as opposed to the dreams they had for me.

It wasn't until I first redefined my Why that I was able to excel and begin my journey to success. Now everything I do, every business decision I make, and even every association I keep has to line up with my Why. If it's taking me away from achieving my Why then I cannot be a part of it. I share my Why with friends, family, business partners and I'll even share it with you as often as possible.

Here's my Why:
1. *To live out my full divine purpose that God has for my life*
2. *To provide abundant permanent provision for my family*
3. *To help change as many people's lives as possible*

Looking at this everyday helps keep me focused and striving toward attaining my goals. Every one of these points **motivates me** through good and especially through bad times. They have **someone other than myself at the center**. They each **make me cry** if I am not actively pursuing them and I am **willing to die for** any of them. That's my why.

More important than "How-to" is "Why-to". Anyone or anything can come along and force you to change your "How-to" but only you can change your "Why-to".

Successful people have a strong Why.

ATTITUDE

Your attitude creates your reality

"Act as if it were impossible to fail"
-Charles Kettering, Inventor

"For as he thinketh in his heart, so is he"
-Proverbs 23:7, Holy Bible

Now that you've developed a strong enough WHY, the next key to unlocking the successful you is your attitude. Not attitude in the sense of how you act around others but attitude in the sense of how you look at situations in your life. Your attitude toward any particular thing will determine your actions toward that particular thing. If someone has a negative attitude towards people of a certain race, gender or religion then history has shown that they will act negatively toward that race, gender or religion. The same goes for a positive attitude. The fact that you're reading this book proves that you have a positive attitude about becoming more successful and improving yourself. There's no getting around it, your attitude creates and drives your reality. If you don't like your reality then you need to change your attitude. As long as you think it's OK to have just enough and you're content with just getting by, then that's the life you'll live. Success can only come, when your attitude changes and you declare, "Enough is enough and I deserve more".

> *Attitude creates and drives your reality*

I must say, by no means am I the first author to write about the importance of a positive mental attitude, and I can assure you I won't be the last; however, if so many experts in the field agree that a positive attitude is important for your success then that's called a clue. The Bible states in Proverbs 23:7 that "As a man thinks in his heart, so is he"; translation, whatever you think, you become. Positive thoughts lead to positive outcomes and negative thoughts lead to negative outcomes. The human mind is the most powerful resource available to man. With your mind you have the power to create your destiny and your future. The root of all your failures and all your successes can be traced right back to your attitude. That's right, a simple change in your attitude can launch you into greater dimensions of success.

Act as if it were impossible to fail

What if you were given a mission to complete and you knew going in that without a shadow of a doubt there was no way you were going to fail? The mission would put you through some of the most difficult obstacles you have ever faced. You may lose your family and friends. You may lose your house, your car, your clothes, your job, everything you own. You may have to fight battles with depression, self-doubt and anxiety. You may go to bed hungry and wake up starving at times. It may seem that all your dreams are fading. You may even begin to feel that God has forsaken you but upon completion of the mission you would be given your every desire. All your dreams would become reality. You would get the keys to your dream home and dream car. Sick family members would be made whole. Your kids would only go to the best schools. You could travel wherever and whenever you desire. You would never have to set your alarm clock for 5:00am to go to work again. Your business, ministry, or organization would prosper abundantly. Words such as "broke", "stress" and "struggle" would permanently erase themselves from your life. Everything you touched would turn to gold. Would you do it? Of course you would; we all dream of a better life free from worry and hardships.

I have some good news and some bad news for you. The good news is that millions of people already live that stress-free lifestyle and God is no respecter of person so if they can do it so can you. The bad news is none of them were guaranteed they would not fail their mission. Many people go through great struggle with no idea what's at the end of the storm. They don't know if they will see brighter days or get blown away. No one is given any guarantees but we all are given the power to choose. Successful people make the choice to *"Act as if"*. They act as if it were impossible to fail. When you choose to act as if it were impossible to fail then that attitude creates your reality and then it IS impossible for you to fail. You will still struggle and you may face some tough obstacles along the way but when you know it's impossible for you to fail, success is not far away.

Four feelings that affect your attitude

Many times we're told to have a positive mental attitude but never taught what elements contribute to our positive or negative attitude. You may be surprised how many negative people actually believe they have a positive attitude and outlook on life. Personal Development Guru, Jim Rohn talks about four things that affect your attitude. Since he has now retired meaning some of you will never here him speak (live anyway) I've taken them and added my own twist to them in the hope that you can gain a better understanding of how our attitude is developed.

1. How do you feel about your past?
It can be said that your past generally serves as the foundation upon which your attitude is built.

> *You can't live your entire life bearing the guilt of past mistakes*

Whether your past is positive or negative is not the primary issue but rather how you feel about your past. There are many people with horrible past experiences that still manage to pull the positives out of those experiences. Jim Rohn said to learn from the past not live in it. The world is full of "Rags to Riches" stories and none of them were by accident. You can't live your entire life bearing the guilt of past mistakes. You can't keep blaming your current destructive actions and poor decision making on the fact that your momma raised you and you never knew your "real" daddy. Believe me, for every sad story about your life someone has a story that can top it ten fold. Let go of the pain of the past and trust in the promise of the future. Learn to find the silver lining in every grey cloud from your past.

2. *How do you feel about your future?*

Successful people look back for education but look forward for inspiration. Learn from the mistakes and accomplishments of your past and be inspired by what tomorrow holds. If you don't have something to look forward to or there's not a mark you're pressing toward then you are living a useless and wasteful life. God put every single one of us here to fulfill a purpose and quite frankly, that excites me. To know that God chose me and trusted me enough to fulfill a goal He set makes me excited about what the future holds.

When you can see where you're driving it's a lot easier to get there than trying to navigate through the fog. Successful people have only positive thoughts about their future. They have goals and plans for their career, education, family, spiritual life, relationships, and so on. Decide what you want and write it down. Start checking things off as you accomplish them and watch how as the checks grow so will your positive feelings about your future.

3. How do you feel about everybody?

Successful people learn quickly that they need the help of others in order to be successful. How you feel about others plays a great role in developing your attitude. Learning to trust people contributes to a positive attitude toward other people. However, trusting people is often easier said then done. What was one of the first lessons our parents taught us as children? "Don't talk to strangers." What did they do when you brought a bucket full of candy home on Halloween? Checked it for "poison". Ever heard "Don't trust 'em as far as you can throw 'em"? Our entire life we're taught, and sometimes for good reason, not to trust people and over the course of 30, 40, 50 years that affects our attitude and is very difficult to overcome. It is essential that we learn to develop positive relationships with others so we may build the trust needed for a positive attitude.

4. How do you feel about yourself?

Self-confidence is a bare bone necessity for success and a positive attitude. If you don't believe in yourself why should anyone else believe in you? Self-confidence helps you take giant leaps toward your goals and aspirations. There will be times when everyone is against you and doubting your every move but you have to be confident enough in yourself to go forward anyway. Confidence enables you to do what you set out to do without being afraid of making mistakes and learning from them. Don't get self-confidence confused with being cocky or arrogant. Confidence means you believe you can do it. Arrogance is when you believe you can do it and because of that you are better than everyone else. Self-confidence is to positive as arrogance is to negative. When you can feel good about your past, good about your future and good about everybody else, you should have no problem feeling good about yourself.

Positive Affirmations

If you've lived in America for any period of time between the late 1980's and early 1990's and watched television on Saturday night then surely you've been introduced, whether directly or indirectly, to the Saturday Night Live character, Stuart Smalley. Stuart Smalley was a psychiatrist type with a daily affirmation segment that ended with the line, "I'm good enough, I'm smart enough and doggonit, people like me". While SNL made fun of affirmations and those that use them, the most successful people in the world have been known to recite positive affirmations as a part of their daily activities. Affirmations, although corny to most average people, play a significant role in the lives of most successful people.

> *"I'm good enough, I'm smart enough and doggonit, people like me"*

Just what is a positive affirmation? In their book *Self-Talk, Self-Affirmation & Self Suggestion*, Paul J. Meyer and John Gardner Jr. define an affirmation as *"A positive declaration stated in the first person and in the present tense that describes specifically what you want to be, what you want to do, what you want to have, and/or how you want to live your life."* God says to "speak those things that be not as though they were" and "the power of life and death are in the tongue". If an affirmation is good enough for God than doggonit it's good enough for me. God didn't say think those things that be not; He said "Speak". That means there must be some power in *saying* positive affirmations.

> *Decide, Determine, Declare*

So how do you create a positive affirmation? You must **Decide** what you want or where you want to be in life, **Determine** what needs to change to get you there, and **Declare** it to be so. Let's look briefly at all three:

#1 Decide

Take an honest inventory of your life and compare it to your dreams and goals. Decide which goals have yet to be accomplished and make a decision to reach them. Let's say you dream of one day buying a home. The decision you would make is to buy a home.

#2 Determine

Determine what parts of your life need improving, what bad habits need to be eliminated, what actions need to be taken in order to get you there. In our example, you may determine that you need to improve your credit score, save more money and spend less. This will serve as the foundation of your affirmation. You must take those factors and transform them into positive statements in the present tense. Be as specific as possible with each affirmation.

"I have A-1 credit and lenders are begging to give me money."
"I save 20% of my paycheck every week and still have surplus."
"I am a responsible spender."

#3 Declare

After you've decided what you want and you've determined how to get it, all that's left is to declare it. An affirmation isn't worth the paper it's written on if you don't say it out loud everyday and declare it to be so. The more you declare your affirmations, the more you'll begin to believe them. You'll subconsciously begin to live and act as if it was already done. The more you declare your affirmations the more positive your attitude will be and the more it will reinforce the actions necessary to achieve them.

One final thing about affirmations, they're not magic. You will have to work to make them manifest. Affirmations without actions are like a brand new car without keys, worthless. That car may look beautiful in your driveway and having it may make you feel like a million bucks but you might as well not have it if you can't have the keys. Affirmations are the same way. It's great to say you believe in them and have them posted everywhere but if you're not going to put in the work to make them happen then you might as well not even have them. In the *Success Is In Your Hand Workbook Companion* you will have space for your daily affirmations. You will begin each day of the 21- Day course by writing five positive affirmations and each evening you will write two more. I encourage you, if you have not already, to purchase the workbook companion so you can put to work all that you will learn in this book.

MY STORY

I thank God for blessing me with a positive attitude. Many people have to learn to be positive but God blessed me with an uncanny ability to always keep a positive mindset even in the darkest times. He has used me to motivate and inspire countless people and give them hope when they thought all hope was gone. God has given each of us who believes in His Word the power to dictate our lives simply by the words we choose to speak and the sentences we choose to pronounce on our very life. We have the right to choose our destiny and as my friend and author Katrina Ferguson says in the title of her book, we need to *Celebrate The Power In The Right To Choose.*

I'll admit I was one of those who thought affirmations were corny. I figured I was already positive enough and I believed in myself so why did I need to talk to myself about it. I was to "cool" for some stupid affirmations. I took a look at my life and soon discovered that I was just like every other ordinary Joe and ordinary just wasn't going to cut it. I started studying some EXTRAordinary people and discovered that most of them developed affirmations and spoke them daily. Being rich and successful was much cooler to me than being a broke underachiever so guess what happened. Affirmations became the cool thing for me to do.

My affirmations partnered with my "act as if it were impossible to fail" attitude propelled me to levels of success I didn't even know were for me. I've had material things taken from me and I've had friends and family doubt me and tell me to "get a real job". I've even had financial troubles and fought through many failures. Through it all I knew without a doubt that I could not fail and God had not forsaken me and now ALL my dreams are coming true. And you know what else, I'm good enough, I'm smart enough and doggonit, (some) people like me.

Successful people keep a positive mental attitude.

PERSONAL DEVELOPMENT

*Become the person you want to be
before your business card says you are*

"Most homes valued at over $500,000 have a library.
That should tell you something"
-Jim Rohn, Motivational Speaker

"Study to show thyself approved unto God…"
-2 Timothy 2:15, Holy Bible

One key to guarantee a more successful life is probably the most overlooked and undervalued key. That key is personal development. Developing yourself is very easy to do but the problem lies in that it is very easy not to do as well. The good thing is that this kind of personal development doesn't require a 10-year membership to any gym and you can do it without even breaking a sweat. This personal development is the development of your mind.

Personal Development is critical in unlocking the successful you. Just as it sounds, you want to develop, enhance, grow and expand your mindset, your way of thinking and the way you look at life and interact with others. The purpose of personal development is to increase your value in the marketplace in order to set you apart from everyone else that does what you do.

> *...personal development is to increase your value in the marketplace*

Personal Development is simply being deliberate in making sure that you grow everyday. Once God has shown you what it is He wants you to do then it is your responsibility to become the best you can be at it. Realize I didn't say become *the best* at it but become the best *you can be* at it.

Knowing what you know today is not enough to get you through the rest of your life. Your attitude toward life and your success should be "What can I learn today?" Ninety-nine percent of the people who do what you do won't read a book today or listen to a self-help audio program that would benefit them. That one small behavior over a period of time will put you leaps and bounds ahead of the other 99%. Successful people are like sponges soaking up as much knowledge about their profession or industry as they can hold. They continue learning until they grow to the level that they can be "wrung out", pouring out all they have into the lives of others.

Personal Development is the one thing that has changed my life and has given me the order and focus that I lacked. Read further, and I promise that the application of the following concepts will change your life forever as well.

STRENGTHS AND WEAKNESSES

As you evaluate yourself through your personal development you will begin to discover your strengths and your weaknesses. Knowing your strengths and weaknesses is key to becoming successful simply because it takes significantly more energy, work and pain to be successful in an area that you are weak. For example, being an accountant, while not impossible, will definitely be a difficult career choice if you hate math, have a hard time paying attention to detail and get bored easily. However, building a career in an area compatible with your strengths will propel your career and lead too much greater levels of success. Far too often I see people jump into careers that they are not best suited for simply because that's the hot industry or it is paying the most money. The key is to find your strengths, develop those strengths through education, experience, books, seminars and trainings and aim to become the best you can be at what you do well. As you continue to develop yourself, you will set yourself apart from everyone else and then the opportunity for success will come to you instead of you chasing after it.

Your strengths are given to you for a reason. Believing that we are all put here to fulfill a divine purpose, we must understand that God has instilled in each of us certain strengths to help us live out our assigned purpose. Think about what things come natural to you, things that emphasize your strengths. Are you a good cook? Are you good at organizing things? Are you athletically gifted? Are people naturally drawn to you?

For me leadership, writing and speaking come naturally. All of my life these three elements have played a prevalent role in my development. From being captain of the football team in high school to being senior class president in college, to now running four businesses, I have always been in a leadership role. In high school I was placed in Gifted &

Talented English and was only one of a handful of students who earned a perfect score on the Maryland Writing Exam in the 9th grade. I've been a songwriter since college and now am a published author. Writing has always been an important form of expression for me. Finally, there is speaking. God blessed me with a strong deep voice, growing up I always thought it was so I could be the cool bass singer in an R&B group like Mike McCary from Boyz II Men. It wasn't until I listened to God that I realized my voice was to be used to educate, empower and equip today's leaders. I enjoy speaking. I rarely get nervous from being in front of a crowd (That in itself is a feat). I have spoken to groups as large as 17,000 people at one time and it felt great. So what is it for you? What strengths do you possess that will make you wealthy, prosperous, and successful?

Your strengths are your ticket to a successful and abundant life. Building your life around your strengths is not only enjoyable but also very rewarding. Foster your strengths, take them seriously and use them. Pray to God for Him to show you your strengths and what they are to be used for and He will do it. There's nothing worse than knowing your strengths and using them for the wrong reasons. Even if it's a good reason, if it's not your divine purpose you still will never reach your full level of success.

Now let's discuss weaknesses. Generally throughout time there have been two trains of thought when it comes to dealing with personal weakness. Thought #1: Find your weaknesses and work on them so you can get strong where you are weak. Thought #2 (and the one I and most successful people subscribe to): Find your weaknesses and get people who are strong in those areas to fill them for you. Why in the world would you waste precious time and energy to fight a battle that you are already losing before you even begin? Working on your weaknesses not only takes you away from your strengths but it in turn makes you non-productive. Let me take this time to clarify one thing, I'm not talking about personality weaknesses, like being an evil person (I'll talk about that later in this chapter), but I mean physical tangible weaknesses that can be measured. If you are poor in time management then it makes more sense to get someone strong in it to help you schedule your daily tasks, even if you have to pay them. If you can come up with great ideas but cannot seem to get people to act on them then you lack leadership, find a great leader who can get others to act on your vision as you focus on the next task.

> *Your strengths are your ticket to a successful abundant life.*

John C. Maxwell says, "No great accomplishment was ever achieved by one person alone." You are going to need help from others regardless of what you do. Doesn't it make sense then to get help from others where you are weak and grow where you are strong? When you get others to fill your void eventually their knowledge becomes your knowledge. That new knowledge works to strengthen your weaknesses. You become stronger and your success does not suffer because you stayed focused on your strengths and not your weaknesses. However, if you try to overcome your weaknesses on your own eventually you may get strong, but you will have lost time and weakened in areas you were once strong because you left those areas neglected. Consequently, a vicious cycle begins of building weaknesses and nothing ever gets accomplished. Success is never achieved. Being weak in an area is not a bad thing; however, being weak and not properly addressing it will be detrimental to your success. Find your strengths and weaknesses and deal with them properly.

THE PERSONAL DEVELOPMENT PUZZLE

There are four pieces to the personal development puzzle that will help you measure your progress in your own personal development.

1. *What goes into you*

What you let in you is the number one determining factor of what kind of person you will become. If you keep filling your body with junk foods and sugars you will inevitably become an overweight person. Your attitude on life, they way you treat others and the decisions you make are all signs of what mental foods have gone into you. Remember when your mother use to say "If you don't have anything nice to say then don't say anything at all?" Does it sometimes feel like your mother was the only one that ever taught that? How often has someone said something negative to you about your dreams, career goals or hobbies and because of their comment you changed your course? Too often we allow people to plant little seeds of discord and doubt in our minds and justify our silence by saying we didn't want to start any trouble. The next time somebody starts a conversation with you with those infamous six words, "I don't mean any harm but..." you need to stop them right there, start some trouble and not let that negativity into your mind. Once you let those negative thoughts in it's sometimes impossible to get them out.

While significant portions of harmful things do get into us from others, we are still responsible for the majority of the "junk food" our mind is forced to filter through. Instead of spending your next 10 minutes of free time reading the latest novel from John Grisham or E. Lynn Harris maybe try some Mark Victor Hansen or John C. Maxwell. Instead of watching all six hours of Sports Center or the Real World Marathon try watching The Discovery Channel or The History Channel from time to time. Instead of the same songs on the radio all day or the latest CD try listening to some motivational books on tape.

Of course I don't want everyone to stop having fun and be serious all the time, but you must be careful that those "negative" inputs are used only for recreation and release from stress. They should not be your main source of information for determining how you live your life. So many people complain about not having enough time to be more than they are when in reality its just improper management of the time they do have. If every one of us only has 24 hours in each day then why do some people *make* time to prosper while others *waste* time in poverty? It's how you use your 24 hours that makes the difference. If all you have in each day is two hours of free time then you have too choose if you will use that time to better yourself or belittle yourself. American men spend an average of 80 minutes a week looking for the TV

> *Four Keys to the P.D. Puzzle:*
> 1. *What goes into you*
> 2. *What comes out of you*
> 3. *Associations*
> 4. *Who you become along the way*

remote. That's an extra 6 hours a month. People have made fortunes with an extra 6 hours a month. Get off of the couch and do something. Will you turn on the TV or will you work on your business plan? Will you go bowling tonight or will you attend a seminar or training in your field? These decisions, while at the time seem minor, will play a major role in your level of successful living.

2. What comes out of you

Once you begin to grow inside there will inevitably be growth on the outside. Personal development is something that, in the beginning, only you know is happening but very soon everyone else sees the fruit of your labor. The following six qualities will help you gauge your development.

Personal Image- The way you dress, the way you talk, the way you walk, your personal confidence and your overall appearance all will change for the better as you continue to develop yourself. It is impossible to grow on the inside and not see a change on the outside. As you begin to grow, your self-esteem will increase, your confidence will increase and your belief level in yourself will also increase. Once your image of yourself changes then you will never be able to let someone else tell you what you can't do. It will be impossible for you to settle for mediocre or average when you know you can achieve greatness.

Attitude- Do people like being around you or not? Your bad day is not a free pass to treat others any kind of way. As you grow you learn to not let your personal issues interfere with your relationships with others. Through your personal development you will learn the power of a positive mindset. Little things that use to get under your skin will not bother you anymore because you will be focused on the big picture. Your success is strongly connected to the relationships you build and the influence you have with others. People have to like you if you expect them to want to be around you and help you. The quicker you change your attitude the quicker you will get to your desired outcome.

Adaptability- Do you go with the flow or do you complain about change? Change is a necessary godsend not evil. Just like standing water starts to stink, non-innovative thinkers who fight change are soon forced to look for work elsewhere. Part of the personal development process is understanding that change is good and rather than fight it simply ask how can you help it. Contrary to most of our beliefs, this world will go on with or without us. If we want to have an impact on it then we need to learn to adapt and encourage change. If you keep doing what you've always done you'll keep getting what you've always gotten. If your life is not what you thought it would be then you need to change some things about your life if you expect something different. A great book to help you deal with change is *Who Moved My Cheese* by Spencer Johnson. Read it and it will help you get over all of your hemming and hawing.

<u>*Are you a Taker or a Giver-*</u> Do you bring something to a relationship or do you constantly drain from someone else for your own needs? No one likes to be around someone who doesn't carry his weight but wants everyone to cater to his needs. You should aim to bring more to the table then you take away. Look first to see what you can do for others before you seek what you can get out of a deal. If you spend most of your time trying to reap from the relationships you have and little time sowing into them, eventually, just like a farmer who expects a harvest yet plants no seed you will look up and have nothing. Successful people aren't freeloaders and they do not resort to deceptive tricks to get their way. No one likes to be taken advantage of and your success weighs heavily on how much you give of yourself as opposed to how much you can take from others.

<u>*Vision-*</u> Do you see a brighter tomorrow or are you stuck in yesterday's problems? Successful people are successful because they focus on the solution and not the problem. They focus on the destination not the twists and turns in the road. Vision enables you to see the final result before the

methods of achieving the result have even been conceived. If you stay focused and help others see the promised land through your eyes and get them to attach themselves to your vision, you will be amazed at how much more effective you will be. Vision, however, can get those who have it in trouble because they can see things as if it were right in front of them while others without vision just can't. Vision caused Joseph to be thrown in jail, vision caused John the Baptist's beheading, vision even caused Martin Luther King's assassination. What are you willing to go through to fulfill your vision? People are looking for a cause to fight for, a crusade to embark upon, and a vision to grab hold of to make their own. If your vision is big enough it will draw more than enough people to make you a tremendous success.

Humility- Do you enlarge others or do you belittle them? So many people allow their ego to get in the way of them achieving success. An ego will not allow anyone else to get credit for something you did. An ego will not allow anyone else to feel good about a small task they did when your task is greater. An ego also will not allow you to be nearly as successful as you could be without one. Being humble, making others feel big about themselves and feel like they were even more important than you will pay big dividends when it comes to achieving success. Learning how to empower others will not only make you a more successful leader but it will make the people you lead more successful. In this day and age so many people are caught up in titles and positions. They feel a sense of validation through their title; however, if the title is stripped away what are you left with? Jesus said that "The last shall be first and the first shall be last" so if you are sitting on your high horse mistreating people because they are "beneath" you then I suggest you jump off before God kicks you off. Successful people do not need titles, they need people and the way you get people is to humble yourself and empower others so that everyone has a sense of ownership in the task at hand.

3. Associations

The saying goes "You are the average of your five closest friends". Like it or not you are. Think about the cars your friends drive, the places your friends live, the income of your friends, how many children your friends have. If your friends have dreams you probably have dreams. If your friends are positive you're probably positive. If your friends go to church you probably go to church. If your friends curse you probably curse. If your friends have negative lifestyles you probably have a negative lifestyle. If your friends lie, steal and cheat you probably lie, steal and

> *You are the average of your five closest friends*

cheat. I think I've made my point. The point is many of us need new friends.

There's another old saying "Guilty by association". Accept it or not, you are judged by the people you hang around. As you begin to grow in your personal development realize one thing, light and dark cannot coexist. Some associations you'll have to limit and others you'll have to break all together. As you grow, your current friends will either grow with you or you will outgrow them. I'll let you know now so you're not surprised when it happens, they probably won't grow with you. So you have to choose what's more important- your current state of reality having just enough to survive or the possibility of abundant success and prosperity in the land of more than enough.

Don't let your "friends" sabotage your dreams with words like "I'm just keeping it real" or "I'm not being negative I'm being realistic." What's real is what's right now; living check to check, working all day everyday to make ends meet, running from creditors, working a job you hate, spending only five hours a day with your family between 6pm and 11pm only to go to sleep and wake up and do it all over again tomorrow, that is today's reality. Who wants to live like that for the rest of their lives? Your dreams of abundant success are not a real possibility to your friends so they feel that it cannot be real for you either. The devil is a liar. If your friends want to "keep it real" by keeping you right where you are then that's a clear indication that that association must be destroyed. If you try to keep the friends that are trying to keep you from moving forward then I can promise you that you will never find the success that has eluded you.

4. Who you become along the way

Have you ever been told, "You have so much potential?" I personally hate that. Potential is good but more important than what is in you is how much of that you can get out of you. So many people feel like having potential is all they need in order to be successful, but have you ever seen a tombstone read "COULD HAVE BEEN A LOVING MOTHER" or "WOULD HAVE BEEN A DEDICATED FRIEND"? Of course not! Life and success is not about what you tried, it's about what you DO. From this day on take the saying "At least I tried" out of your vocabulary. That's a submission to failure and it has no place in a successful persons mind. If trying was all it took to be successful then where would this world be? What if Thomas Edison, Carter G. Woodson, Harriet Tubman, Barry Bonds, Garrett A. Morgan, Madame C.J. Walker, Bill Gates, Sam Walton, Mary Kay Ashe, Rosa Parks or countless other trailblazers all settled for "At least I tried"? It was through learning from failures and giving their best that they overcame obstacles and became great successes in their fields. It was through those very failures that those individuals grew to the level of notoriety and respect that they are given today.

The subtitle of this chapter says "Become who you want to be before your business card says so." You have to grow into the position before you're in it. You have to read now what those who are where you want to be are reading, go where they go, do what they do so when opportunity knocks you're ready to open the door. Natural skill and ability can only get you to the door but you have to grow to a certain level to be able to kick the door in. When you submit to personal development and make it a part of your everyday life, in one week you'll be addicted. In one month you'll start saying things and wonder, "Did that come out of my mouth?" And in one year you'll ask, "How in the world did I get here?"

STAY TRUE TO THE PROCESS

Staying true to the process can be very difficult to do when you're in the middle of it. Hindsight is 20/20 but when you're in the midst of the storm it's all shades of gray. Look at it this way, if Donald Trump or Oprah Winfrey wrote you a check for $10 Million and they gave you a laundry list of things you had to do in order to cash the check, what on that list, as long as it was ethical, wouldn't you go through? It's the same way with God; He has signed over to you a blank check granting you access to all the success in the world but there is a list of things you must do and go through in order to grow to where you can handle the success He has for you. Surely God could snap His fingers tomorrow and give you everything you have ever prayed for, but who would benefit from that other than yourself. The process we go through is so much bigger than just us, the process enables us to learn about ourselves and become more than we ever thought possible so that we may turn around and help others with what we have gained.

> *Every successful person must go through the growth process*

Every successful person must go through the growth process; there is no short cutting it. Embrace it and learn from it because you will need to share your story with others who will follow in your footsteps. If you have never overcome failure then how can you teach someone else to overcome failure? If you were never dead broke and overcame it then how can you empathize with someone who is in that situation and help him or her get out. Don't get angry with God for putting you through a test. Go through it and thank Him that He chose you to go through it in order to use your experience to help others. Once you have gone through your process you will be able to lead others by example and not by theory. Successful people grow and teach through real life applications not through hypothetical theory. Don't be afraid to fail because in each failure you will find a lesson that will get you closer to success. How you deal with failure, hardship and the overall process will determine the success you become and the impact you will have in the lives of others.

MY STORY

In April 2001 I was properly introduced to the Network Marketing Industry. I, like many, had heard of the industry but always had a negative opinion of what I heard. It wasn't until I met a group of down-to-earth gentlemen from Maryland, Darnell Self, Antonio Adair and Michael Humes, that were making more money in a month then I was making all year that I was able to really appreciate what was before me. These guys looked like me, but they did not talk like me. These guys were where I was from, but we were going two different places. These guys had the same dreams I had, but theirs were becoming reality. They had everything I was striving for, the financial freedom, time freedom, houses, cars and the ability to help others so when I asked them how do I get what they had I was shocked by the answer.

They didn't say go and sell 5,000 widgets and wonder sprays, or recruit the entire nation and I'll be rich, they said "Read a book." That's the essence of personal development. I had to have a shift in my mindset before I could see a shift in my paycheck. Knowing the "how-to" is good for mediocrity but knowing the "why-to" is essential for success. Personal development is simply changing what goes in you so that it changes what comes out of you.

> *I had to have a shift in my mindset before I could see a shift in my paycheck*

When I got started in Network Marketing I had never read a "Self-Help" book (I had never read any book from cover to cover for that matter). The first book I read in its entirety was John C. Maxwell's *21 Irrefutable Laws of Leadership* and just like they said, it changed my life. My library is now growing daily and I feel like I still don't have enough books. It was the personal development that helped me to grow into the success before the success was documented. It was personal development that gave me more knowledge and insight on business, leadership and working with others than the majority of the managers of major corporations. (Ask your boss what's the last good book they read)

Personal development is what gave me the confidence to pursue my dreams. It was personal development that made me unemployable at the age of 26, helped me to walk away from my job and I have never have a boss since. Once your mind has been expanded, it is impossible to shrink it back.

Personal development is as necessary to your success as oxygen is to human life. But here's the thing, when I began my personal development I began to outgrow my friends, some people I just couldn't hang around as much and some people I couldn't hang around at all. I wasn't trying to be mean and I'm still friends with everyone, but now I have limited associations with those who don't have what I want and aren't actively doing what it takes to get it.

I realized in order to get something different I had to do something different. If I didn't start my growth process when I did there is no way I'd be where I am today. I'll say it again; knowing what you know today is not enough to get you through the rest of your life. You must constantly learn and grow each day.

Successful people constantly seek personal development.

Ryan C. Greene

BELIEF

*If you don't believe in yourself
why would anyone else believe in you*

"The future belongs to those who believe in
the beauty of their dreams"
-Eleanor Roosevelt, Former First Lady

"For we walk by faith, not by sight"
-2 Corinthians 5:7, Holy Bible

When it comes to belief, there are two types of belief necessary for your success. The first is your belief in God's promises. You have to believe that God has called you and has purposed you to be successful and prosperous. You have to believe that what He says is true and that it applies to your life. Secondly, you must believe in yourself. You must believe that you are chosen to succeed and that you can achieve anything you set your mind to. You must believe that nothing can come between you and a successful life but you.

> *It is God's desire that His people are successful*

Let's begin with God's promises. It is God's desire that His people are successful. We are created in His image so for us to live anything less than an abundant and prosperous life is contrary to His intention for our lives. The problem many people face is they do not understand that God's promises come with ground rules. There is a standard that God has set for anyone to be eligible for His promises. God does not lower His standards so that it can fit us, but we must raise ourselves and grow to acceptable levels so that we can fit His standards. You can't just live any kind of way and treat people however you please and expect to be rewarded by God. His promises are real to those who believe and submit to the standards He has set.

I want to share with you just a few of my personal favorite promises from God. After each verse I will share some insight on what God is saying and what that promise means to the individual seeking success. I guess I better warn you beforehand; once you read these promises from God, you can never again say you did not know how greatly God wants to see you succeed in life. Let's get to the verses:

> *"I know the plans I have for you," declares the Lord,*
> *"plans to prosper you and not to harm you,*
> *plans to give you hope and a future."*
> *-Jeremiah 29:11*

The Lord will grant you abundant prosperity. The Lord will open the heavens, the storehouse of his bounty, to send rain on your land in season and to bless all the work of your hands.
-Deuteronomy 28:11-12

Beloved I wish above all things that thou may prosper and be in health, even as thy soul prospers.
-III John 2

And he shall be like a tree planted by the rivers of water that brings forth his fruit in his season; his leaf also shall not wither; and whatsoever he does shall prosper.
-Psalm 1:3

I am come that they might have life,
and that they might have it more abundantly
-John 10:10

Isn't it great to know that God not only wants you to prosper, but He has already made the plans for you to do so?

God informs us that His plans are not to harm us but to help us prosper. He will open the heavens and provide everything we need exactly when we need it. He promises to bless the works of our hands and bring prosperity to whatever we do. God has already set things in order for you to live an abundant life and He's just counting on you to do the work.

Doing the work is the hard part. The work serves as your testing period and your purification process. It is where your true colors shine. In 1 Corinthians 10:13, Paul writes that God will not allow you to be tempted by more than you can handle or bear. Most people give that scripture a negative connotation but it also relates to your blessings and prosperity. God is not going to put you through more hardship than you can bear but He also will not give you more prosperity than you can bear. God knows that most people are not mentally, emotionally, spiritually and physically able to handle the temptations that come from success so He forces us to mature in those areas before He allows success to overtake us.

God's timing and man's timing do not always match up but God's timing is always right. Some people have to work for months while others may have to work for years to prepare themselves for God's purpose for their life. Let's explore how God advises us to handle our testing period:

Blessed is the man who perseveres under trial, because when he has stood the test, he will receive the crown of life that God has promised to those who love him.
-James 1:12

Do not fear, for I am with you; do not be dismayed, for I am your God. I will strengthen you and help you; I will uphold you with my righteous right hand.
-Isaiah 41:10

The Lord will keep you from all harm-He will watch over your life; the Lord will watch over your coming and going both now and forevermore.
-Psalm 121:7-8

You will call, and the Lord will answer; you will cry for help, and He will say: Here am I.
-Isaiah 58:9

The eyes of the Lord are on the righteous and His ears are attentive to their cry
-Psalm 34:15

I think it is safe to say that God rewards those who persevere. God lets us know upfront that there is going to be a test of your will power and faith, but if you only hold on He will see you through. God has promised you the crown of life just for withstanding your trial. He also said not to fear or be dismayed. He will strengthen and uphold you when you are weak. Fear is not of God so you need to eliminate it whenever it tries to pop up in your mind. God ultimately says in Psalm 121, "I got your back". He promises to watch your coming and your going and He also hears your cry.

Even in your wilderness experience, when everyone else has abandoned you, God will not forsake you. He said, *"You will cry for help, and I will say: Here am I."* Why is Here capitalized? It is capitalized to represent God. God *is* Here. Wherever you may find yourself, God, in his omnipresent way, is Here. He is an ever-present help. You don't have to worry whether or not He's busy doing something else or if He's checking the Caller ID and avoiding your calls. You don't have to wait in line or set an appointment. God is ever-present and He's got your back.

Finally, it's time to look at what you need to do. God has promised you prosperity and He said He would never leave you nor forsake you. He did His part and now it is up to you to do yours. What are some of the conditions of God's blessings?

Delight yourself also in the Lord;
and He shall give you the desires of your heart
-Psalm 37:4

But seek ye first the kingdom of God, and His righteousness;
and all these things shall be added unto you.
-Matthew 6:33

Commit your works unto the Lord,
and your thoughts shall be established
-Proverbs 16:3

If they obey and serve Him, they shall spend their days in prosperity, and their years in pleasures.
-Job 36:11

Then shall you prosper, if you take heed to fulfill the statutes and judgments, which the Lord charged Moses concerning Israel: be strong, and of good courage; dread not, nor be dismayed.
I Chronicles 22:13

But thou shall remember the Lord thy God: for it is He that gives you power to get wealth, that He may establish His covenant which He swear unto your fathers, as it is this day.
-Deuteronomy 8:18

If my people, which are called by my name, shall humble themselves, and pray, and seek my face, and turn from their wicked ways; then will I hear from heaven, and will forgive their sin, and will heal their land.
-2 Chronicles 7:14

It is pretty clear that God is not in the business of just giving away blessings. If He simply allowed us to walk in our destiny and purpose without earning it then we would take the credit for God's work. But He has things set up so that when you abide by His rules, you can't help but to give Him the glory for your success. Think about it, most people would be more grateful and appreciative of $50 that they worked all day for than if someone just gave them $100 for doing nothing. The same holds true for success. You will appreciate and value your success and the promises of God more when you go through something to attain them.

> *God is not in the business of giving away blessings*

God wants us to delight ourselves in Him. That means we get joy from doing His work and *then* He will give us the desires of our heart. He wants us to first seek His kingdom and righteousness. We cannot put anything before Him, not our job, business or even family. We must seek Him first and *then* all things will be added unto us. He wants us to commit our works unto Him. We must commit all that we do to God so that He may be glorified and not man. Once we commit our works to God our thoughts are manifested and brought to life. In order to spend our lives in prosperity, we must obey and serve Him and take heed to fulfill His statutes. Finally, we must humble ourselves, pray, seek His face and turn from our wicked ways. Then God promises to forgive our sins and heal our lands.

What land in your life needs healing? Is it your finances, marriage, business, or your mind? God has promised you many things; success is one of His major promises to you. God cannot lie. If you believe your success lies within Him then great things are in store for your life. Show your belief by holding God to his word. Do what He says and watch Him keep His Word concerning you.

> *If you do not believe in yourself than why would anyone else believe in you?*

Your second area of belief has to be the belief in yourself. If you do not believe in yourself then why would anyone else believe in you? No one can force you to believe in yourself. The fastest way to improve your belief in yourself is to jump in the water and start kicking. If that's too much, you can build up your self-confidence through little successes and gradually work your way up.

You will find it near impossible to achieve significant success without first believing you can achieve it. Let me give you my formula for Belief: VISION + FAITH = BELIEF. It all starts with a Vision. You have to see your life play out before anyone else can see it. Right now you may be a stockbroker or a stock boy but you can still see yourself achieving great levels of success in your lifetime. Your current situation does not have to be your permanent destination. Vision allows you to see the finished product before the plans have even been drawn up. Helen Keller was quoted as saying, "I would rather be blind and not see than to have sight without vision."

> *VISION + FAITH = BELIEF*

Next, you add Faith. Faith is the substance of things hoped for and the evidence of things not seen. It is that substance and that evidence which gives you faith that your vision will come to fruition. Faith is a powerful force. It allows you to speak those things that are not as though they are. It gives you power to move mountains. Faith is what powers your vision. Your faith has to be in someone bigger than you. God gives you the vision and in turn you give God your faith. When you combine vision and faith, you have belief. Vision is birthed in your mind and faith is birthed in your heart. Your heart tells your head what to do and your head tells your body. That is the manifestation of Belief. When you believe strongly enough in something, you begin to act on it.

Big Vision plus Big Faith equals Big Belief. Little vision plus little faith equals little belief. I am giving you 19 keys to unlocking the successful person God designed you to be but if you do not believe that you can be successful than the other 18 keys do not even matter. Don't be afraid to dream the biggest dreams. God has purposed you to be successful so do not short-change Him. Dream bigger than you have ever dreamed before. Dust the cobwebs off that vision you once had for your life. Have faith in God that He will supply your every need. Believe in yourself and act as if it were impossible to fail. The actualization of your dreams is not dependent upon others belief or support in your dream. It all depends on your belief.

MY STORY

One night in January 2003 I was awakened from my sleep by a still voice that spoke only three words to me. The voice said, "You are chosen." I knew without a doubt that God was speaking to me to comfort me in the midst of a very turbulent time. Those three words assured me that the troubling journey I was on was orchestrated and predestined by God specifically for me. I was facing some of the toughest crises in my life and was beginning to second-guess my call, my decision-making and my purpose. My belief was waning. I could not figure out why nothing seemed to work out for me. Every time I could barely peak my head above water to catch a breath another tidal wave would wash in and overtake me. It was that night that my vision met up with a new stronger faith and my belief has never faded since.

The storms did not cease that night in January, but all of my doubts met a swift and vicious death. Learning that God had chosen me, promised me success and prosperity and had not forsaken me gave me great comfort in a time of distress. I began to really look into God's word to find out just what He wanted from me. I began to discover what my role was in fulfilling my destiny and how I could accelerate my process. It was then that I learned that God is not in the business of giving away blessings. I had to increase the work I put in toward serving Him as well as increase the work I put in to fulfilling my purpose.

God assured me that anything I did would succeed if I only dedicated it to Him and put the work into building it. This book is just one testament of that. I never in my wildest dreams imagined I would someday be a published author. I had never even read a book from cover to cover until four years ago. It was because of where He has brought me from and where He is still taking me that I knew it was my responsibility to make sure God was glorified throughout this book.

I could have written this book for the commercial masses and made vague references to God and the Bible in order to ensure a greater mainstream acceptance, however, I know where my blessings come from and I refuse to keep that a secret from anyone. God's stamp of approval is all I need to be successful. As one psalmist put it, "What God has for me it is for me". If He did it for me He will certainly do it for you. All you have to do is BELIEVE.

MORE KEYS TO UNLOCKING YOUR SUCCESS

So far I've discussed developing your strong Why and three major keys to unlocking the successful you. In this chapter I will discuss 15 other keys that will help you unlock your success. Each key is important and will have a great impact on your life as you master them. John C. Maxwell said that "Leadership doesn't happen in a day, it happens daily" and the same can be said about success. It's impossible to read this book one time and expect to have the success you are looking for by tomorrow, but the daily application of the principles taught will unlock your success over time.

These 15 keys are like the combination to your lock in that all 15 are necessary and equally important. The good thing is that the order in which you apply them doesn't matter, just as long as you apply them. As you go through this chapter you will discover that each key could have an entire book to itself, however for the sake of space I'll stick to just a page or two for each one. More in depth teachings are available through my website www.ryancgreene.com and at the seminars and trainings that I hold across the country.

These keys are a combination of tasks, qualities, and principles that when put all together will make you a much more successful person mentally, physically, emotionally, financially, socially, and spiritually.

1.) Set Goals & Develop Strategies

Start with the end in mind & Make a plan to get there

A goal is something you desire to accomplish but a plan is your roadmap to achieving that goal. There are five points that a good goal must have. First your goal must be Specific. The more specific your goal is, the easier it is to focus on it. Secondly, your goal must be Measurable. You need a way to determine if you're moving in the right direction toward your goal. Next your goal must be Action-Oriented. You have to put forth a plan of actions that will move you toward achieving your goals. If you don't work toward reaching your goal then you will never reach it. Goals do not just come true because you hope they will. Fourth, your goal has to be Realistic. Losing 50 pounds in 2 weeks is not a very realistic goal. Losing 2 pounds a week for 50 weeks is much more realistic. Finally, your goal has to be Time Sensitive. You can't set an open-ended goal and figure you'll achieve it whenever. Eighty percent of the work on any project gets done in the last 20% of the time. If you don't have a date to reach your goal then you'll never reach more than 20% of your goal.

Now that you have properly set your goals, it's time to develop your plan to achieve it. There are six easy questions you should ask yourself to help develop your plan. Question #1: "WHO do I need help from?" Thinking you can do everything all by yourself is the fastest way to fail at anything. Question #2: "WHAT are my landmarks along the way?" You need landmarks to be sure you're on the right path and on pace to reach your goal. If in January you have a goal to earn an extra $10,000 this year a landmark would be to earn $5,000 by July. Question #3: "WHERE will I get the resources to achieve my goals?" The money, supplies, equipment, training and even time has to come from somewhere. Question #4: WHEN will I start and when will I finish. Question #5: "WHY do I want it?" Probably the most important question, this will serve as your motivation to keep going. And finally, Question #6: "HOW will my life be different if I achieve my goal and how will it be different if I don't, and which result am I willing to live with?"

2.) Become A Better Leader
Would you follow you?

In today's society everyone wants to be called a leader. In business you'll find companies with 100 Vice-Presidents and only 30 employees. In church everyone is "Bishop" now and sometimes the bishops don't even oversee one church let alone a group of churches (as the name implies). The sad reality is great leadership is extremely hard to come by. If everyone is leading then who is following?

Leadership can be simply defined as "the ability to influence others to do something they otherwise wouldn't have done had you not asked them to". It is inevitable that at some point in your success journey you will need to get people to move toward a goal you have, and becoming a better leader will be necessary to achieve that. Ask yourself, "Who's following me?" now ask, "Would I follow me?" Answer yourself honestly so that you can evaluate your current level of leadership. When I asked myself those question years ago I realized that most of the time I didn't even do what I told *myself* to do so how could I expect others to do what I said and follow me.

Often times people feel they are good leaders because other people follow them, but a closer look may reveal that they lead subordinates or only people that look up to them. This may make them a leader in the raw sense of the word but it certainly does not make them a great leader. A great leader transcends all levels and barriers. If you only lead people that are younger than you, or the same race or religion as you, or the same or lower social status as you then you have some growing to do in your leadership. I reference Martin Luther King Jr. a lot because he was an example of a great leader. At the age of 26 when he started, he was able to rally all races, religions, age groups and social classes to abolish racial discrimination and change how an entire country is governed. That's great leadership.

As a leader, you attract what you are. Leaders are drawn to better leaders. The better leader you become, the better leaders you will attract. Leadership is not in a title but it's in your actions. A great leader doesn't need a title in order to lead. While becoming a better leader there are two goals you need to focus on: learning from other great leaders and developing great leaders of your own.

3.) You Must Have A Burning Desire
I'll do it or I'll die

Burning: Increasing fury

Desire: Conscious impulse toward an object or experience that promises enjoyment or satisfaction in it's attainment

Successful people have a burning desire. When you look at the definitions of the two words it really brings it into perspective. You must have an increasing fury toward attaining success because of the satisfaction its attainment will bring. Successful people have the attitude that there is nothing that will quench that desire but the fulfillment of their dreams or goals. As you search for your ticket to success, an easy way to determine if you're heading in the right direction is by measuring your desire to do it. God's not going to call you to do something you aren't driven to do. Even if you try to run from your called purpose, the desire still remains.

God said to seek His kingdom and He will give you the DESIRES of your heart. I have a burning desire to impact and change the lives of others in a positive way. That burning desire pushes me to write more books, have more speaking engagements, give more seminars, train more people and build more businesses. Even when my physical energy is low and depleted, it's a burning desire that keeps me going. What do you have a burning desire to achieve? What is it that makes you say, "I'll do it or I'll die"? That's the thing right there. That's the key to your success. Focus your energy and resources toward that thing which you have a burning desire for and watch how things begin to change in your life. Watch how success will begin to chase you down.

4. Be Coachable

If you already know it all then why don't you have it all?

Michael Jordan is arguably the greatest basketball player ever to play the game. Throughout his career he won 6 NBA Championships, 6 NBA Finals MVP Awards, 5 League MVP Awards, had 13 All-Star Game appearances, 3 All-Star Game MVP Awards, is the NBA's third all-time leading scorer and has countless other records and awards. Michael Jordan clearly was an expert at what he did but amazingly enough in light of all of his accomplishments, he still had a coach. Why would "His Airness" need a coach? What could he stand to learn from anyone else? The answer is simple; sometimes a different set of eyes can see what you can't see. When Jordan had an off night it was Phil Jackson's eyes that could tell him he didn't have full extension on his jumper or he wasn't bending his knees on his free throws. What if Michael Jordan thought he knew it all and there was nothing more he could learn? How great would he have really been? The same principle applies for you in your field. Until you're the one teaching, and even once you are the one teaching, you need to always be learning.

The ability to humble yourself and be willing to learn from others will get you to greater levels of success much higher and much quicker than those who do not practice humility. No one likes a "know-it-all" and successful people don't strive to attain that title. In order to be successful in what you do, you should strive to learn more everyday. Finding mentors who have done what you want to do and following in their footsteps makes much more sense than trying to reinvent the wheel and do things your way. A true expert in any given area isn't an expert because they *know* all the answers but rather because they know where to *find* all the answers.

The day you begin to think you've 'arrived' and no one can teach you anything is surely the day you will see your success begin to dwindle away. Success comes to those who are humble and are always seeking to learn more.

5.) Build Positive Relationships

It takes help from others to achieve success

We all have heard the saying "It's not what you know but who you know" and quite honestly that statement still rings true. My first published article and even my first radio interview were both done for people I already knew and with whom I had built positive relationships. You'll find it very difficult to get ahead of the pack by being an obscure, silent, mysterious character. People need to know you and you need to know them as well.

Positive relationships can be relationships with people with similar goals as yours, people with positive attitudes and mindsets, or even positive professional working relationships. Keep in mind you don't have to be best friends with everyone but your goal should be that whenever your name comes up in a conversation it brings a smile to a person's face. You want people to feel good about working with you so they'll be willing to help you when you need it.

One good way to start building these relationships is through networking events. These events, perhaps a luncheon, a meeting or happy hour, enable you to meet a variety of people and exchange business cards in the hopes of doing business. This is a great way to get your name known in the business community and build significant contacts.

Another great way to build new positive relationships is by attending seminars and trainings in your area of expertise or interest. Seminars and trainings not only help you learn about particular topics but they allow you to meet people who share your common interests and goals. Finding someone in the same field to work with can have many positives for the both of you.

Finally, joining an association will definitely lead to building positive relationships. There are literally hundreds of thousands of organizations throughout the country. I can almost guarantee you'll be able to find one that fits your field. Go online and do some research and find an association to join. Associations not only give you access to people but you'll have access to industry specific information, workshops, meetings, certifications, other resources and the built in credibility that comes from being a member. Most associations charge membership fees or dues to join but the price you will pay for not joining is much more costly than the price you will pay to join.

The bottom line is people do business with people they know and trust. Networking, attending seminars and joining associations are three great ways to meet new people and form successful alliances.

6.) Stop Listening To Negative People

If they don't have what you want then their opinion doesn't matter

Who is your dream killer? In 1993 Willie Jolley told my freshman class at Hampton University to stay away from dream busters. I cannot tell you another thing he said but that one thing has stuck with me all these years and I hope it sticks with you. How often have you bounced an idea off of someone and they said it wouldn't work or you couldn't do it? Or how about those people who can't find a positive thing to say about anything? Negative people will find everything wrong with an idea and focus on why it won't work instead of finding the positives and thinking what if it does work. The reality is that most negative people cannot see *themselves* succeeding so they displace that negative attitude on others and disguise it with sayings like "I don't mean no harm but…" or "I don't want to see you get hurt".

Negative people are like plagues, even worse they are a mental parasite slowly eating away at your mind destroying all of your success cells in order to make you into another loser like them. The only fortunate thing about the disease of negative people is that there is a cure. STAY AWAY FROM THEM! Too many people destroy their lives and accept failure all because they are worried about what others will think. Too many dreams are lost forever because would-be successful people abort their dreams prematurely due to complications brought on by friends and family.

Why would a married couple only go to single people for marriage counseling? Why would a Christian go to an atheist to ask about salvation? Why would a success driven person who wants more out of life go to a negative, dream stealing, bad attitude having, always complaining, complacent underachiever for advice on how to get ahead just because it's your husband, your mother or your best friend? If you want success and would like to free your mind of the negative influences attacking it then you must be firm in your resolve to stop listening to negative people. Remember, if they don't have what you want, and aren't trying to get it, then their opinion doesn't matter.

7.) Understand That A J.O.B. Doesn't Work

<u>If your name's not on the building, then you're building someone else's dream</u>

This key may surprise a lot of people but J.O.B.s simply don't work. I guess I should preface that statement by saying that this key is only for those who desire to be financially wealthy as part of your model for success. Maybe you've heard it before but a J.O.B. stands for "Just Over Broke". Again, this key is not for everyone and please don't go and quit your job tomorrow. Everyone doesn't want to be rich but for those who do, this is for you.

Let's start with this, put in your mind a picture of your dream home, your dream car, your dream vacation spot, your dream wardrobe, and your dream income. Now ask yourself who at your job has any of what you just pictured. Anyone? OK, whom do you know that at least does what you do and has any of your dreams? Anyone yet? How about whom do you know that has *any* job and has what you dream of having? Pretty hard, huh? Get the picture? That's why jobs don't work. It's not that jobs are bad but they just weren't designed to make you wealthy. How many times have you worked a job you hated just to make ends meet? The thing about two ends are that they never meet and if they ever were to meet then you would be going in circles.

Would you rather work a job or own and create jobs? Statistics show the average American income from a job is $26,000 while the average American income from a home-based business is $50,250. Successful people always have a "Plan B". The 'B' in this case is Business. Just by owning your own home-based business you can lower your income tax bill by $3,000-$7,000 a year before you even make your first sale. Creating an additional profit-center for your household, regardless of the income amount, not only allows you to live a better lifestyle but it also gives you options about your future, relieves financial stress and builds self-confidence.

How many times must you watch people get laid off or downsized before you realize that there must be a better way? Don't get me wrong, everyone can't own a business (and not everyone should try) or else who would work, but if you want real security and financial success then there is room for you. I have watched countless individuals say, "It can't happen to me" and yet they were still downsized, laid off, fired, their company goes under, or the company restructures to streamline management and their left looking for work. Too many people put all of their eggs in one basket and don't even realize the basket has a hole in it.

If you cannot control the future of the hands you are putting your future in then that's a problem. Find out what you are good at and what your gifts are and get the help you need to build that into a business. A job should be used to gain experience and knowledge, not as your sole source of money. A job should be your stepping stone into your destiny not the stumbling block that keeps you from ever reaching your destiny.

8.) Be Of Good Character And High Integrity

<u>*What people think, IS important*</u>

One of the easiest things to lose and yet the hardest thing to get back is your good name. Successful people learn this early on and understand how important character and integrity are to achieving success. In life, it doesn't matter how trustworthy you think you are or what a caring person you believe yourself to be. What matters is how others perceive you in those areas. What others perceive to be true about you is their reality about you regardless of how true or false their perception may be. It is crucial that the perception you think you're giving off matches the perception you actually give.

Good character can be summed up as the qualities you possess. How do you treat people? Are you trustworthy? Are you easy to be around? The morals and values that govern your life will shape your character. Something as small as just being on time can have a major impact on your character in the eyes of others. You don't want to be known for always showing up late for everything. Some people may see you as irresponsible or untrustworthy. Once someone labels you it's almost impossible to erase that label. Learning to be more conscious of things you say and do and thinking more about how your actions affect others will help you to develop a favorable character among others.

High integrity is your uncompromising adherence to a code of moral value. Having values and standing by them speaks volumes about a person. Successful people don't lie, steal and cheat to get to the top. Having integrity means you do the right thing even when no one else is around. It means your word is your bond. If you say you're going to do something then you get it done. People want to work with people they can trust and the more people who trust you, the larger your network of available resources grows, the larger your network of resources grow; the larger your success grows.

9.) Help Change Someone Else's Life
If you're not changing lives you need to change your focus

Keon Terrell White was a 23-year old man who the news never did a story on. Keon wasn't a drug dealer, hip-hop thug, or a professional athlete; he was a student at Howard University. Keon was in Howard's Fine Arts Program and was on his way to Oxford University in England until he was killed in a car accident in June of 2003. I never met Keon and I don't know all the details of his death but I was at his funeral because his brother Darrell attends my church. I witnessed person after person, young and old, attest to the greatness of this young man and the impact he had on their lives. The lives he touched were clearly changed forever. Many of the college students rededicated their lives to Christ and gave up bad habits and even I now strive to touch the lives of others in a more positive way all from what others said about someone I never even met. "Live Life" was the motto he lived by and in his short yet complete life he changed countless other lives.

One third of my life mission statement is to change as many lives as possible. The whole purpose of this book is to change someone's life. My goal is to help you become more successful after reading this book then you were before you read it. I get such fulfillment from the thought that something I said or wrote or some decision I made turned someone in the right direction and made his or her life better. Successful people understand the more you give then the more room you have to receive. Your sacrifice alone could be the one thing to change someone's life.

Zig Ziglar says, "People don't care how much you know until they know how much you care-about them". When you can make other's goals a part of your goal instead of keeping them apart from your goals then you have mastered this key and are on your way to unlocking your success. Successful people are constantly looking for ways to help others and improve more then just their own life.

10.) Write Things Down
<u>A free mind will lead to FREEDOM</u>

One of my biggest challenges has always been remembering all the things in my mind I have to do. My mind is always racing with new ideas, places I need to be, business ventures I want to explore and most importantly my shopping list for Wal-Mart. It wasn't until a few years ago when I started writing things down that I began to see a tremendous difference in my productivity. Once I began writing things down I could free those thoughts from my mind and clear that space for something else. Many of us clutter our minds with unnecessary garbage thereby leaving no mental capacity for us to just think and use our mind for more important matters.

One quick and easy way to relieve some of the stress in your life is by putting your thoughts on paper. This way you don't forget that next million-dollar idea you have and you can go back to it whenever you want. Have you ever had a great idea and two hours later you couldn't remember what it was?

With technology today you don't even have to write them down, you can record them. My cell phone is full of 15-second messages of things to do or lines for a book or whatever else comes to mind. Once I get the thoughts down I can relax and move on to the next thing.

Your mind dictates your actions. If your mind is stalled because it is full of unorganized thoughts then your life will reflect that through your actions and also stall. On the contrary, if your mind is clear, open and free then you will soon realize a life of freedom.

11.) Ask Questions

<u>People can only help you when they know you need help</u>

"The only dumb question is the one not asked." Ever heard that before? I know a few people who seem committed to dispel that theory. I'm not saying they ask dumb questions but they sure do push it. The thing about questions is no matter how out of right field some may seem; they are still necessary. I would much rather ask questions, regardless how off the wall they may be, and ensure I have a total and complete understanding than to let my ego get in the way and try to figure it out myself. Asking questions let's others know that you are smart enough to know when to seek help and that you care about getting better.

Successful people never stop asking questions. It's through questions that you grow and improve yourself. If you ever get to the point where you aren't asking questions any longer than one of two things has happened; 1) You have stopped growing because you think you know all there is to know or 2) No one is asking for your advice anymore because they see you have stopped growing and you think you know all there is to know. Regardless of how successful you become, you can always get better. The quickest way to get more is to ask those that have more how to get it. You are reading this book because you have questions on how to unlock the successful person God designed you to be and by asking that question, hopefully by this point, you have gained much more than you had when you first picked up the book.

So I guess that old saying is right, there really is no such thing as a dumb question. Right?

12.) Take Action

<u>The road to hell is paved with good intentions</u>

The difference between potential energy and kinetic energy is that potential energy is the energy stored up and kinetic energy is the actual energy in action and working. Your potential for success is great, however, you must take action, or become kinetic, in order to access your potential. How much potential you have stored inside is not as important as how much of it you can get out. All your hopes, dreams, promises and plans don't mean a thing if you don't take action and work toward them.

It seems simple enough and like it would only make sense but taking action is really where many people get hung up. People spend a lot of time and resources making plans but it takes courage and commitment to put those plans to work. It takes courage to make that first prospecting phone call or to write and implement that business plan. It takes guts to walk away from a comfortable job to pursue something new and uncertain, but taking action is the only way to overcome your fears of failure. I cannot promise you will not fail if you take action, but I can promise if you do not take action you will fail every time.

God has not given us the spirit of fear and yet it is that very emotion that keeps people frozen in the land of "What-Ifs" afraid to step into their destiny. Taking action means you are going to have to get rid of your friends "Shoulda", "Woulda" and "Coulda". Taking action means you are going to have to jump out of your comfort zone. Taking action means you are going to have to deal with and overcome the bumps and bruises of life. Taking action means you have to "Just do it".

Most importantly, taking action means you are taking steps toward unlocking the successful you.

The lights and the camera are ready and now it's time for you to take action!

13.) Be Committed To The Process

Go all out or go home

Becoming successful is a process. There is a divine order in which events must occur in order for you to reach the place God wants you to be. Along the way you will encounter obstacles and roadblocks that you must overcome. You will have people come and go in and out of your life. You will have days when you feel like you are on top of the world and other days when you feel like the whole world is on your shoulders. There will be some tough decisions you will have to make and certainly some sacrifices along the way. Success does not come easy but it does come to those who stay true to the process.

Successful people are like oysters that have a tiny piece of sand caught in their shell. The oyster lives on the ocean floor surrounded by sand yet it is able to keep the sand from entering its shell, however every now and then a piece of sand gets lodged inside the oyster's shell. That sand causes the oyster severe irritation and discomfort. The oyster must fight through the pain of the sand in its shell and find a way to overcome that difficult period. The oyster uses it own power within to fight the sand by covering it in calcium and proteins until finally a pearl is formed. The oyster has gone through a tough period in its life but because it transformed a negative situation into a positive one, it is now the most precious creature in the sea.

As individuals, troubles surround us on all sides just like the sand does the oyster. Hard times will come but it's up to us to make pearls out of every situation. Each person's process may be different but yours is the exact process that you need to go through. I never claimed achieving success would be easy, if that were the case there'd be no need for books on the subject, however knowing that if you just stick things out then success is inevitable enables you to appreciate the process and learn from it. Knowing there is a process you must go through and staying committed to it by not trying to shortcut your way to success will keep you focused and ultimately lead you to victory.

14.) Make The Most Of Every Day

Am I better today than I was yesterday?

Life is a minute, Only 60 seconds in it, Forced upon you,
Can't refuse it, Didn't choose it, But its up to you to use it,
You must suffer if you lose it, Give an account if you abuse it,
Just a tiny little minute, But eternity is in it.

One of the biggest problems that I see people wrestle with is overcoming procrastination. People waste far too much time with insignificant activities when that time could be used fulfilling their purpose and having a greater impact on the world. Time is our most precious and valuable commodity and up to this point no scientist or scholar has figured out how to get it back once it's gone so it's important to use every minute you have wisely. It's important as you work toward unlocking your success that you understand the importance of time and become a good steward of it. A successful person's goal is to always be better today than they were yesterday.

What do Bill Gates, Oprah Winfrey, Donald Trump, Sam Walton and You all have in common? The answer: God gives each of them 24 hours a day. No one gets a single nanosecond more yet four out of the five listed are Billionaires. The first four made a decision to make the most out of everyday and to milk everything they could out of every minute while they were building their success. How much TV do you think Bill Gates watched when he was creating the largest software company in the world, Microsoft? How many bowling nights did Oprah Winfrey go to while she was building one of the most powerful media empires in the world, Harpo? How much sleep do you think Donald Trump got when he was buying half of the real estate in New York City? Do you really think Sam Walton was just hanging out with the fellas when he built Wal-Mart? Now what about you? What are you willing to give up in order to be the next success story? When are you going to start taking life seriously and stop wasting the time God blessed you with and use it to do what He put you here to do? Successful people are willing to do now what others don't so later on they can have what others won't.

Statistics show that the average human lifespan is 79.5 years. That means if you're 20 years old, you have about 700 months left to live. If you're 30 years old, you have about 600 months left. A 40-year-old person has about 480 months left to live and a 50 year old has about 320 months left to live. When compared to the eternity of God and to the 30-40 Billion years of Earth's existence, even 700 months seems like but a minute. Unfortunately we were not given the luxury of deciding how much time we have, nor can we put life in reverse and take advantage of the time we let pass us by, but each day we can make a decision as to how we will spend those 24 hours. It is that daily decision that when life is all said and done will leave you saying either, "I sure am glad I used my time wisely" or "I wish I would've used my time more wisely".

Your destiny is waiting on you. It's waiting on you to make a decision to stop dreaming about your purpose and start walking in it. Turn off the TV, cancel guys' night out, skip bowling this month and do something productive with all that time you "don't" have. Future generations are depending on you making the most out of today so they may have a better tomorrow. The average person only has 300-700 months to make their impact on the world, don't let yours waste away.

15.) Don't Ever Quit

It is impossible to stop a man or woman who will not quit

In 1969 The Baltimore Colts faced the underdog New York Jets in the NFL's Super Bowl 3. The New York Jets were led by a young Joe Namath and were the inferior AFL team. Many were shocked when Joe Namath guaranteed a Jets victory over the Colts. The Colts were coached by Don Shula and were the clear favorites to win. That game went down as the "Greatest upset of all time" as the Jets defeated the Colts 16-7. After the loss, Don Shula was ridiculed, practically blacklisted and ultimately fired by the Colts.

Surely dejected and feeling down, Don Shula could have quit coaching, but he didn't. Don Shula went on to coach the Miami Dolphins where he went to three straight Super Bowls, won back to back Championships in 1973 and 1974 and led the Dolphins to the only undefeated season in the history of the NFL. The coach that was once ridiculed and suffered the greatest upset of all time went on to become the winningest coach in the history of the NFL and is known as one of the "Greatest Coaches of All-Time".

For Don Shula quitting was never an option. Even when everyone was against him and told him he didn't have what it takes to succeed, he believed in himself and became more successful than any other coach in the history of the NFL. Quitting cannot be an option for you either. No one is going to give you success on a silver platter. You are going to have to scratch and claw to get it. You are going to have to believe in yourself when no one else does.

There is a price to pay for success but when it's all said and done, there is also a price to pay for not succeeding. If your Why is strong enough and you apply the keys taught in this book, the only thing that can stop your success is quitting. As one of my mentors Michael Humes always says, "It is impossible to stop a man or a woman who will not quit." Too many lives are attached to your success. There are people that are waiting for you to finish your race in order for you to help them through theirs. When you quit, you are not just quitting on yourself but you are quitting on all the people depending on you to press on.

Ryan C. Greene

YOUR GAME PLAN

FOR SUCCESS

Now it's time to go to work. Throughout this book I have given you my 19 keys to unlocking the successful you. Now it is time to bring it all together by giving you a game plan to put into action that which you have learned. All of what you have learned is worthless if you do not have a game plan for implementing it into your life. I have given you the playbook and now here is the game plan to unlock the successful you. There are 12 Action Steps that will serve as your plan of action to ensure your success. This game plan combines aspects of the 19 keys for unlocking the successful you with easy to do behaviors that will get you started right.

Your Game Plan For Success
1. *Decide To Be Successful*
2. *Determine Your Why*
3. *Discover Your Vehicle*
4. *Develop Your Goals and Strategies*
5. *Duplicate Someone Who Has Already Done It*
6. *Daily Positive Affirmations*
7. *Daily Personal Development*
8. *Desire To Be The Best You Can Be*
9. *Don't Dodge The Process*
10. *Destroy All Doubt*
11. *Don't Waste Time*
12. *Don't Ever Quit*

1. *Decide To Be Successful*

Your first step is to make the decision to be successful. No one ever says they want to fail but millions of people make that decision every day. Making the decision to be successful is more than simply saying you want to be successful. It requires a resolve within you to be willing to go through the journey necessary to reach success. Deciding to be successful also means you refuse to allow any negative forces and influences to penetrate your positive mental being. No one is going to force you to be successful. You have the power to choose what kind of life you will live. Whether you realize it or not, every decision you make is either a decision to be successful or a decision to fail. How you spend your time, money and resources are all decisions you make to either fail or succeed. Decide to be successful by making successful decisions. Once you make an honest decision to be successful, then it is time for Step 2.

2. *Determine Your Why*

Once you have decided to be successful, the next action is to determine your WHY. Most people will never experience the overwhelming emotion of hoisting a championship trophy above their head as their team wins it all. To feel the joy that comes with knowing you have reached the climax of an epic journey makes all you went through worth it because for this moment in time you are the best. The training camp, the off-season workouts, the weight training and conditioning, the grueling season, the triumphs and the defeats, the negative press saying you couldn't do it, the time away from family, it was all worth it. That trophy is a physical manifestation of all the effort and energy you invested into your success.

Every season every team believes this is their season to win the championship but in the end there is always only one team left standing. The only thing that keeps the other losing teams coming back next year is their dream of holding up that trophy. They can deal with everything the season throws their way by simply staying focused on the trophy.

Your Why is your "trophy". It is your physical or mental motivator that propels you toward success. Your Why has to be in the forefront of your mind at all times. When you are pushing through your storms, your vision needs to be so focused on your Why that you cannot even worry about the How. When you develop a big enough Why, God will take care of the How.

3. *Discover Your Vehicle*

Success is not some hocus pocus mojo where you just sprinkle some magic pixie dust and "Voila!" you are everything you want to be. Success takes work. You have to put something in to get something out. Therefore you need a vehicle that will serve as the platform for your success. By vehicle I don't mean a plane, train or automobile but your occupation, profession or vocation. Your vehicle is simply, what you do that garners your success. Selecting the right vehicle is extremely important to your success. It is so important that God has already selected it for you. You simply have to ask Him to show you and direct your path toward it.

Don't fall into the trap of trying to be successful in a field that you were not purposed for. Someone else's success in a given area does not guarantee yours. Your vehicle may be education, entrepreneurship, writing, singing, mechanics, cleaning, preaching, accounting or any one of millions of professions. The key is to discover YOUR vehicle. Once you discover your vehicle, then expand it and maximize it. Explore every opportunity available within your vehicle. Figure out how you can get the most out of what it is you do, how you can impact the most lives through your vehicle, and how you can help and empower the most people coming up after you.

4. *Develop Your Goals and Strategies*

Once you have discovered your vehicle, it is time to lay out your goals and strategies. Your goals will include what you hope to gain and accomplish. Your strategies are your detailed plan on achieving your goals. There is a familiar saying, *"If you fail to plan, you plan to fail"* which proves that your plan is very important in reaching and achieving your goals. Refer back to Chapter 6 for information on exactly how to set good goals and develop strategies that will work. I can't stress enough the importance of goals. Your goals are your vision and without a vision you are fighting a losing battle. Every successful person has goals as well as strategies to achieve them. Be purposeful about your goals because success does not happen by accident.

5. Duplicate Someone Who Has Already Done It

What is the easiest way to get what you want? Find someone who has already *ethically* done it and do what he or she did to get it. In school we were always taught to do our own work and not to copy. We were punished and called cheaters for getting help from someone more skillful than us. But in the real world "cooperative learning" will get you a lot further a lot faster. I was once told, "It's OK to be a copycat just as long as you copy the right cat". I'm not talking about cheating or stealing from others but I'm talking about finding mentors and other successful people who are willing to share with you what they did to become successful.

Why do you think the NBC show *The Apprentice* was such a huge hit? One million people auditioned for a chance to learn business from Donald Trump. Every contestant stated that it was an opportunity of a lifetime to learn from one of America's most successful business icons. How much faster could you reach your goals if you had the Donald Trump of your industry teaching you step by step how to do what he or she did to become successful? I spent four and a half years in college and amassed over $74,000 in student loan debt because I wanted to learn how to start and run my own business. Imagine how surprised and dismayed I was when I realized that all of my instructors' had PhD at the end of their names but not one had CEO. Don't misunderstand me, I received a great education, I just feel I could have gotten a much better, and less expensive, business education from business owners. A mentor can accelerate your growth and guard you from the pitfalls that they have already experienced. A man that findeth him a mentor has foundeth him a good thing.

6. Daily Positive Affirmations

What better way to begin and end each day other than reciting positive daily affirmations to yourself? The world will feed you more than enough negative thoughts and images to process and discard each day. You must take personal responsibility for feeding positive thoughts to your mind. I can promise you that every day will not go as you planned and sometimes life will flat out stink. So who is going to pick you up and urge you to keep going? Who is going to be the good angel on your shoulder saying, "You can do it"? Who is going to pick you up from the muck and mire called life? You.

It is your responsibility to monitor what goes into your mind on a daily basis. The best, time-proven method to maintaining a positive outlook on life and developing high self-esteem is speaking positive affirmations to yourself on a regular basis. One time here and there is not going to do it. It has to be a regular behavior that becomes second nature. The more you speak it, the more you believe it. The more you believe it, the more you become it. The more you become it; the more success becomes you.

7. *Daily Personal Development*

The more you know the more you grow. I don't know if that's an old saying but it should be. Since I devoted an entire chapter to personal development, I don't need to spend too much time on it again. Keep in mind that you can only get out of you what you have already put in you. See yourself as an empty bank account in need of a daily deposit. The more deposits you make the more valuable you become. Personal Development is like your Rainy Day Fund; you never know when you will need it but you feel much more secure knowing it's there. Personal Development improves not just your knowledge but also your confidence, ability and skill level. It helps you become a better person and prepares you for your inevitable success. Your position in life today is a direct result of decisions you made five years ago. Where you end up five years from now will be determined by the decisions you make today. Make the decision to invest in daily personal development and watch what happens five years from now.

8. Desire To Be The Best You Can Be

This book is designed to help you reach your *full* potential and get out of you *all* that God has put in you. It does God, the world and yourself no good for you to just be OK, average or good enough. The world is saturated with average people that are just good enough. Millions of people take their untapped gifts and talents to the grave never knowing what could have been. Successful people desire to be the best they can be. Do not get tripped up in trying to be the best, but push to be the best *you* can be. Being the best you can be has nothing to do with anyone else. You are not competing with anyone but yourself to be the best you can be. Being the best you can be means when it is all said and done and it is time to take an inventory of your life, you can honestly, without a doubt, say you left it all on the field and had nothing left to give. The desire to be the best you can be cannot be taught. You have to acquire it. It is that desire to be the best you can be that will push you further than the average person could ever go.

9. Don't Dodge The Process

What would happen if you mixed flour, baking soda, raw eggs, sugar, butter, vegetable oil and water in a bowl and ate it? You would probably get very sick and at the very least have to fight to keep it down. What if you took that same concoction and instead of eating it you put it in the oven for 40 minutes? Now you have a wonderful yummy cake. What's the difference? The process. Life is just like baking a cake in that you will have all kinds of ingredients coming together to make you. Some will be good like sugar and others will be not so good like raw eggs but when you put them all together and add a little heat to it, everything turns out great.

Everyone's process is going to be different but rest assured, everyone has a process. Have you ever heard, "If you can't stand the heat get out of the kitchen?" The intensity of the heat you are able to endure is an indicator of your growth through the process. A cake has to be baked at 375 Degrees because it cannot handle 400 Degrees. The same is for you. God will not give you more than you can bear so stand firm and don't run from your process. Think about the importance of the process you go through. Your trials and tribulations are the heat that molds and shapes you into a successful person. Some trials may not even be directly for you but never lose sight of the importance of your process. There is something God is trying to get out of you and only the fire can purge it. Success does not come by just going through the process but from *growing* through the process. Successful people don't look for shortcuts around the process.

10. Destroy All Doubt

Once you have committed to the process and are willing to go through your wilderness, the next action step is to destroy all doubt. There will be times when you just don't know what to do next and you have no idea how you are going to make it. It is in those times that you must have faith and belief in God, yourself, and the process. If you have just one percent doubt, you're out.

Doubt has no place in a successful person's psyche. If you have properly planned your steps and you are walking in divine order then where does doubt fit in? Doubt is an enemy of success that must be met head on and destroyed. Doubt is simply fear repackaged. God has not given us the spirit of fear so whenever you feel doubt trying to creep in ask yourself three questions: 1) Have I properly prepared for this moment? 2) Am I following God's purpose for my life? 3) If I answered, "Yes" to one and two then, what am I afraid of?

Believe it or not, some people are actually afraid of being successful. They doubt that success is really for them. They eventually sabotage their life by listening to every excuse of the enemy as to why they are not good enough or why they cannot succeed like others. Doubt is a dangerous enemy that, when left alone, will not only destroy your purpose but it will spread among all those around you. Doubt is not your friend. When you feel it coming you must destroy it immediately.

11. Don't Waste Time

Have you ever felt like there just aren't enough hours in a day to get things done? Does it seem like your To-Do List gets longer each day? Is your middle name Procrastination? Perhaps your problem is not the lack of time but the lack of time management. Let me give you one piece of advice that will help you better manage your time. Throw away your To-Do List!

A To-Do List is one of the worst enemies to a successful person. In order to gain better time management, successful people go from a To-Do List to a Schedule. What good is a laundry list of things to do if you have no plan for when you need to start and complete each one? Most people make a To-Do List with the goal to complete it sometime today, but a schedule spells out what to do, when to do it and how long it should take to do it. Scheduling your time is much more effective than just going through each day doing things whenever you get to them.

Your To-Do List is your starting point; unfortunately the majority of people also make it their ending point. Your goal is to create a daily schedule for yourself that will ensure you take advantage of every minute. Once you list everything you hope to achieve (To-Do List), you have to assign priority to each task. Starting with the highest priority, determine how long it will take you to complete that task and what time you will start. Put that task in your planner and continue through your list doing the same thing for each task. You have now created a schedule. Sticking to your schedule and handling the highest priority tasks first will improve your time management and help you minimize wasted time.

12. Don't Ever Quit

The final step in your game plan is; Don't ever quit. Be patient along your journey and do not get discouraged when things do not go just as you planned. God has already promised your success but it's up to you to remain steadfast and unmovable along the way. No great feat has ever been accomplished without overcoming some type of struggle and the same is true for achieving success. Never quitting is what makes successful people so special.

It may be easy to pack your bags and count your loses when the road your treading gets rough. But it is difficult to live the rest of your life as a quitter wondering what might have been.

Right now your storm may seem too treacherous to weather and it is hard to keep going but life will be much easier and more peaceful once you unfold your potential and are walking in your destiny. It takes a special individual to go against the grain of common logic and to never quit.

Each challenge in your life represents a fork in the road to success. It is at your crossroads where a life-altering decision must be made. Do I quit or do I go on? Do I live a comfortable life now and spend my twilight years uncomfortable or do I deal with the discomfort now and spend the rest of my life in comfort? Ninety-seven percent of people choose comfort now and end up paying for it down the line while only three percent choose to deal with the pain now to live a lifetime of comfort.

People around you are not going to understand why you keep trying different businesses, going after lofty dreams, or will not get a "real" job, but those same people, five to ten years from now, will not understand why you are living the lifestyle they could only dream of living. The only difference between the 97% and the 3% is that the 3% never quit on their dreams. Remember, success does not happen in a day, it happens daily.

Conclusion

While I hope you have enjoyed reading this book, it was not primarily designed to entertain you. The purpose of this book was to educate, empower and equip you with the intangibles necessary to reach greater levels of success and to fulfill your God given purpose. It is my goal to change as many lives as possible and I pray that this book has caused you to make the decision to change your life.

I have given you the tools and the blueprint for success but it is up to you to build the house. How successful do you really want to be? Words may say it but your actions will tell the true story. What you decide to do with the information in your hand will determine how successful you become. One hundred years from now, will people still be thanking you for your contributions to the world or will your impact be a distant far-gone memory?

God has a purpose for your life and it is your birthright to be successful. Make this the last day you ever settle for less than you have been promised. Stop waiting for approval from others for you to be successful. Erase all of your doubts and conquer your fears. You now have the keys to unlock the successful person you were designed to be. Your destiny is waiting on you. Success is in your hand.

WORKBOOK COMPANION

Dear Friend,

Congratulations for making a commitment to unlock the successful person God designed you to be.

This Workbook Companion will be your 21-Day Success Coach. Experts say it takes 21 days to form a habit. As you walk through this workbook and complete the daily exercises, you will begin to form the successful habits taught in *Success Is In Your Hand* and by the end of the 21 days, they will become second nature and a regular part of your life.

Too often people write "feel-good" books or give empty "Rah-Rah" speeches saying, "You can do it, you can do it!" but they give you no substance upon which to grow. It is my intention with this book and workbook companion to not only motivate you but also to educate, empower and equip you with the tools needed to become more successful in every aspect of your life.

I pray you find these books to be a great resource as you continue to unlock the successful you. I also pray for your continued success and the full realization of your divine destiny and purpose.

Success Is In Your Hand.

Your Success Coach,

Ryan C. Greene

Introduction

This workbook is your chance to put into action all of the lessons you've learned in *Success Is In Your Hand: 19 Keys To Unlocking The Successful Person You Were Designed To Be*. Each day you are given a new key to embrace and focus on. You will also begin and end each day with positive affirmations and personal development. Each morning you will list goals for the day pertaining to that day's key and each evening you will reflect on your progress and growth for that day. You will also get in the habit of writing your WHY every morning when you start your day and every evening when you end it.

Your WHY is the fuel that will keep you going and is the most important element to unlocking your success. Because your WHY is so important, developing your WHY is the first step in the 21-Day process. As I explained in the book, there are four questions you need to answer for yourself to develop a strong enough WHY. Those four questions are: 1) What motivates you? 2) Who is at the center of your why? 3) Is it strong enough to make you cry? and 4) Is it worth dying for? Once you've honestly answered those questions, you should have a WHY so strong that no obstacle will be able to come between you and your success. Take a few minutes to do that now in the space provided below.

1. What motivates me?

_____

_____

2. For whom am I living my life? Whose life am I trying to change?

_____

_____

3. What goals will make me cry if I don't achieve them?

_____

_____

4. What am I willing to die for?

_____

_____

MY WHY

_____

_____

_____

Day 1

Morning

Today's Key: WHAT IS SUCCESS TO ME

My Why: _____
_____

Daily Affirmations:

I _____

I _____

I _____

I _____

I _____

Personal Development

This morning I read 10 pages of: _____

Or I listened to 30 minutes of: _____

Five things I can do between today and this time tomorrow that will help me grow in today's key and become more successful.

1. _____
2. _____
3. _____
4. _____
5. _____

Two ways I can use today's key to sow into someone else's life and dreams today.

1. _____
2. _____

Evening

Daily Reflections

What three things did I do very well today? In what area was I most successful?
1. _____
2. _____
3. _____

What one thing will I do even better tomorrow?
_____

What was the most important lesson I learned today about today's key to unlocking my success?
_____
_____
_____

Personal Development

This evening I read 10 pages of: _____
Or I listened to 30 minutes of: _____

Affirmations (Write two new affirmations that you've discovered during the day)

I _____

I _____

My Why _____
_____

Day

1

Day 2

Morning

Today's Key: MY WHY

My Why: _____
_____

Daily Affirmations:

I _____

I _____

I _____

I _____

I _____

Personal Development

This morning I read 10 pages of: _____

Or I listened to 30 minutes of: _____

Five things I can do between today and this time tomorrow that will help me grow in today's key and become more successful.

1. _____
2. _____
3. _____
4. _____
5. _____

Two ways I can use today's key to sow into someone else's life and dreams today.

1. _____
2. _____

Evening

Daily Reflections

What three things did I do very well today? In what area was I most successful?
1. _____
2. _____
3. _____

What one thing will I do even better tomorrow?
_____

What was the most important lesson I learned today about today's key to unlocking my success?
_____
_____
_____

Personal Development

This evening I read 10 pages of: _____
Or I listened to 30 minutes of: _____

Affirmations (Write two new affirmations that you've discovered during the day)

I _____

I _____

My Why _____
_____

Day 2

Day 3

Morning

Today's Key: ATTITUDE

My Why: _____
_____

Daily Affirmations:

I _____

I _____

I _____

I _____

I _____

Personal Development

This morning I read 10 pages of: _____

Or I listened to 30 minutes of: _____

Five things I can do between today and this time tomorrow that will help me grow in today's key and become more successful.

1. _____
2. _____
3. _____
4. _____
5. _____

Two ways I can use today's key to sow into someone else's life and dreams today.

1. _____
2. _____

Evening

Daily Reflections

What three things did I do very well today? In what area was I most successful?

1. _____
2. _____
3. _____

What one thing will I do even better tomorrow?

_____

What was the most important lesson I learned today about today's key to unlocking my success?

_____

_____

_____

Personal Development

This evening I read 10 pages of: _____

Or I listened to 30 minutes of: _____

Affirmations (Write two new affirmations that you've discovered during the day)

I _____

I _____

My Why _____

_____

Day
3

Day 4

Morning

Today's Key: PERSONAL DEVELOPMENT

My Why: _____
_____

Daily Affirmations:

I _____

I _____

I _____

I _____

I _____

Personal Development

This morning I read 10 pages of: _____
Or I listened to 30 minutes of: _____

Five things I can do between today and this time tomorrow that will help me grow in today's key and become more successful.

1. _____
2. _____
3. _____
4. _____
5. _____

Two ways I can use today's key to sow into someone else's life and dreams today.

1. _____
2. _____

Evening

Daily Reflections

What three things did I do very well today? In what area was I most successful?
1. _____
2. _____
3. _____

What one thing will I do even better tomorrow?
_____

What was the most important lesson I learned today about today's key to unlocking my success?
_____
_____
_____

Personal Development

This evening I read 10 pages of: _____
Or I listened to 30 minutes of: _____

Affirmations (Write two new affirmations that you've discovered during the day)

I _____

I _____

My Why _____
_____

Day 4

Day 5

Morning

Today's Key: BELIEF

My Why: _____
_____

Daily Affirmations:

I _____

I _____

I _____

I _____

I _____

Personal Development

This morning I read 10 pages of: _____
Or I listened to 30 minutes of: _____

Five things I can do between today and this time tomorrow that will help me grow in today's key and become more successful.

1. _____
2. _____
3. _____
4. _____
5. _____

Two ways I can use today's key to sow into someone else's life and dreams today.

1. _____
2. _____

Evening

Daily Reflections

What three things did I do very well today? In what area was I most successful?

1. _____
2. _____
3. _____

What one thing will I do even better tomorrow?
_____

What was the most important lesson I learned today about today's key to unlocking my success?
_____
_____
_____

Personal Development

This evening I read 10 pages of: _____

Or I listened to 30 minutes of: _____

Affirmations (Write two new affirmations that you've discovered during the day)

I _____

I _____

My Why _____
_____

Day 5

Day 6

Morning

Today's Key: MY GOALS & MY PLAN

My Why: _____
_____

Daily Affirmations:

I _____

I _____

I _____

I _____

I _____

Personal Development

This morning I read 10 pages of: _____

Or I listened to 30 minutes of: _____

Five things I can do between today and this time tomorrow that will help me grow in today's key and become more successful.

1. _____
2. _____
3. _____
4. _____
5. _____

Two ways I can use today's key to sow into someone else's life and dreams today.

1. _____
2. _____

Evening

Daily Reflections

What three things did I do very well today? In what area was I most successful?

1. _____
2. _____
3. _____

What one thing will I do even better tomorrow?

_____

What was the most important lesson I learned today about today's key to unlocking my success?

_____
_____
_____

Personal Development

This evening I read 10 pages of: _____
Or I listened to 30 minutes of: _____

Affirmations *(Write two new affirmations that you've discovered during the day)*

I _____

I _____

My Why _____
_____

Day 6

Day 7

Morning

Today's Key: BECOME A BETTER LEADER

My Why: _____
_____

Daily Affirmations:

I _____

I _____

I _____

I _____

I _____

Personal Development

This morning I read 10 pages of: _____

Or I listened to 30 minutes of: _____

Five things I can do between today and this time tomorrow that will help me grow in today's key and become more successful.

1. _____
2. _____
3. _____
4. _____
5. _____

Two ways I can use today's key to sow into someone else's life and dreams today.

1. _____
2. _____

Evening

Daily Reflections

What three things did I do very well today? In what area was I most successful?

1. _____
2. _____
3. _____

What one thing will I do even better tomorrow?
_____

What was the most important lesson I learned today about today's key to unlocking my success?
_____
_____
_____

Personal Development

This evening I read 10 pages of: _____
Or I listened to 30 minutes of: _____

Affirmations (Write two new affirmations that you've discovered during the day)

I _____

I _____

My Why _____
_____

Day 7

Day 8

Morning

Today's Key: BURNING DESIRE

My Why: _____
_____

Daily Affirmations:

I _____

I _____

I _____

I _____

I _____

Personal Development

This morning I read 10 pages of: _____

Or I listened to 30 minutes of: _____

Five things I can do between today and this time tomorrow that will help me grow in today's key and become more successful.

1. _____
2. _____
3. _____
4. _____
5. _____

Two ways I can use today's key to sow into someone else's life and dreams today.

1. _____
2. _____

Evening

Daily Reflections

What three things did I do very well today? In what area was I most successful?
1 _____
2 _____
3 _____

What one thing will I do even better tomorrow?
_____

What was the most important lesson I learned today about today's key to unlocking my success?
_____
_____
_____

Personal Development

This evening I read 10 pages of: _____
Or I listened to 30 minutes of: _____

Affirmations (Write two new affirmations that you've discovered during the day)

I _____

I _____

My Why _____
_____

Day
8

Day 9

Morning

Today's Key: BE COACHABLE

My Why: _____
_____

Daily Affirmations:

I _____

I _____

I _____

I _____

I _____

Personal Development

This morning I read 10 pages of: _____

Or I listened to 30 minutes of: _____

Five things I can do between today and this time tomorrow that will help me grow in today's key and become more successful.

1. _____
2. _____
3. _____
4. _____
5. _____

Two ways I can use today's key to sow into someone else's life and dreams today.

1. _____
2. _____

Evening

Daily Reflections

What three things did I do very well today? In what area was I most successful?

1 _____
2 _____
3 _____

What one thing will I do even better tomorrow?
_____

What was the most important lesson I learned today about today's key to unlocking my success?
_____
_____
_____

Personal Development

This evening I read 10 pages of: _____
Or I listened to 30 minutes of: _____

Affirmations (Write two new affirmations that you've discovered during the day)

I _____

I _____

My Why _____
_____

Day 9

Day 10

Morning

Today's Key: BUILD POSITIVE RELATIONSHIPS

My Why: _____

_____

Daily Affirmations:

I _____

I _____

I _____

I _____

I _____

Personal Development

This morning I read 10 pages of: _____

Or I listened to 30 minutes of: _____

Five things I can do between today and this time tomorrow that will help me grow in today's key and become more successful.

1. _____
2. _____
3. _____
4. _____
5. _____

Two ways I can use today's key to sow into someone else's life and dreams today.

1. _____
2. _____

Evening

Daily Reflections

What three things did I do very well today? In what area was I most successful?

1. _____
2. _____
3. _____

What one thing will I do even better tomorrow?

_____

What was the most important lesson I learned today about today's key to unlocking my success?

_____
_____
_____

Personal Development

This evening I read 10 pages of: _____
Or I listened to 30 minutes of: _____

Affirmations (Write two new affirmations that you've discovered during the day)

I _____

I _____

My Why _____
_____

Day 11

Morning

Today's Key: STOP LISTENING TO NEGATIVE PEOPLE

My Why: _____
_____

Daily Affirmations:

I _____

I _____

I _____

I _____

I _____

Personal Development

This morning I read 10 pages of: _____

Or I listened to 30 minutes of: _____

Five things I can do between today and this time tomorrow that will help me grow in today's key and become more successful.

1. _____
2. _____
3. _____
4. _____
5. _____

Two ways I can use today's key to sow into someone else's life and dreams today.

1. _____
2. _____

Evening

Daily Reflections

What three things did I do very well today? In what area was I most successful?

1 _____

2 _____

3 _____

What one thing will I do even better tomorrow?

_____

What was the most important lesson I learned today about today's key to unlocking my success?

_____

_____

_____

Personal Development

This evening I read 10 pages of: _____

Or I listened to 30 minutes of: _____

Affirmations (Write two new affirmations that you've discovered during the day)

I _____

I _____

My Why _____

_____

Day 11

Day 12

Morning

Today's Key: A J.O.B. DOESN'T WORK

My Why: _____
_____

Daily Affirmations:

I _____

I _____

I _____

I _____

I _____

Personal Development

This morning I read 10 pages of: _____

Or I listened to 30 minutes of: _____

Five things I can do between today and this time tomorrow that will help me grow in today's key and become more successful.

1. _____
2. _____
3. _____
4. _____
5. _____

Two ways I can use today's key to sow into someone else's life and dreams today.

1. _____
2. _____

Evening

Daily Reflections

What three things did I do very well today? In what area was I most successful?

1 _____
2 _____
3 _____

What one thing will I do even better tomorrow?
_____

What was the most important lesson I learned today about today's key to unlocking my success?
_____
_____
_____

Personal Development

This evening I read 10 pages of: _____
Or I listened to 30 minutes of: _____

Affirmations (Write two new affirmations that you've discovered during the day)

I _____

I _____

My Why _____
_____

Day 12

Day 13

Morning

Today's Key: GOOD CHARACTER & HIGH INTEGRITY

My Why: _____
_____

Daily Affirmations:

I _____

I _____

I _____

I _____

I _____

Personal Development

This morning I read 10 pages of: _____

Or I listened to 30 minutes of: _____

Five things I can do between today and this time tomorrow that will help me grow in today's key and become more successful.

1. _____
2. _____
3. _____
4. _____
5. _____

Two ways I can use today's key to sow into someone else's life and dreams today.

1. _____
2. _____

Evening

Daily Reflections

What three things did I do very well today? In what area was I most successful?
1. _____
2. _____
3. _____

What one thing will I do even better tomorrow?
_____

What was the most important lesson I learned today about today's key to unlocking my success?
_____
_____
_____

Personal Development

This evening I read 10 pages of: _____
Or I listened to 30 minutes of: _____

Affirmations (Write two new affirmations that you've discovered during the day)

I _____

I _____

My Why _____
_____

Day 13

Day 14

Morning

Today's Key: CHANGE SOMEONE ELSE'S LIFE

My Why: _____

_____

Daily Affirmations:

I _____

I _____

I _____

I _____

I _____

Personal Development

This morning I read 10 pages of: _____

Or I listened to 30 minutes of: _____

Five things I can do between today and this time tomorrow that will help me grow in today's key and become more successful.

1. _____
2. _____
3. _____
4. _____
5. _____

Two ways I can use today's key to sow into someone else's life and dreams today.

1. _____
2. _____

Evening

Daily Reflections

What three things did I do very well today? In what area was I most successful?

1. _____
2. _____
3. _____

What one thing will I do even better tomorrow?
_____

What was the most important lesson I learned today about today's key to unlocking my success?
_____
_____
_____

Personal Development

This evening I read 10 pages of: _____
Or I listened to 30 minutes of: _____

Affirmations (Write two new affirmations that you've discovered during the day)

I _____

I _____

My Why _____
_____

Day 14

Day 15

Morning

Today's Key: WRITE THINGS DOWN

My Why: _____
_____

Daily Affirmations:

I _____

I _____

I _____

I _____

I _____

Personal Development

This morning I read 10 pages of: _____

Or I listened to 30 minutes of: _____

Five things I can do between today and this time tomorrow that will help me grow in today's key and become more successful.

1. _____
2. _____
3. _____
4. _____
5. _____

Two ways I can use today's key to sow into someone else's life and dreams today.

1. _____
2. _____

Evening

Daily Reflections

What three things did I do very well today? In what area was I most successful?
1 _____
2 _____
3 _____

What one thing will I do even better tomorrow?
_____

What was the most important lesson I learned today about today's key to unlocking my success?
_____
_____
_____

Personal Development

This evening I read 10 pages of: _____
Or I listened to 30 minutes of: _____

Affirmations (Write two new affirmations that you've discovered during the day)

I _____

I _____

My Why _____
_____

Day 15

Day 16

Morning

Today's Key: ASK QUESTIONS

My Why: _____
_____

Daily Affirmations:

I _____

I _____

I _____

I _____

I _____

Personal Development

This morning I read 10 pages of: _____

Or I listened to 30 minutes of: _____

Five things I can do between today and this time tomorrow that will help me grow in today's key and become more successful.

1. _____
2. _____
3. _____
4. _____
5. _____

Two ways I can use today's key to sow into someone else's life and dreams today.

1. _____
2. _____

Evening

Daily Reflections

What three things did I do very well today? In what area was I most successful?
1 _____
2 _____
3 _____

What one thing will I do even better tomorrow?
_____

What was the most important lesson I learned today about today's key to unlocking my success?
_____
_____
_____

Personal Development

This evening I read 10 pages of: _____
Or I listened to 30 minutes of: _____

Affirmations (Write two new affirmations that you've discovered during the day)

I _____

I _____

My Why _____
_____

Day
16

Day 17

Morning

Today's Key: TAKE ACTION

My Why: _____

_____

Daily Affirmations:

I _____

I _____

I _____

I _____

I _____

Personal Development

This morning I read 10 pages of: _____

Or I listened to 30 minutes of: _____

Five things I can do between today and this time tomorrow that will help me grow in today's key and become more successful.

1. _____
2. _____
3. _____
4. _____
5. _____

Two ways I can use today's key to sow into someone else's life and dreams today.

1. _____
2. _____

Evening

Daily Reflections

What three things did I do very well today? In what area was I most successful?
1. _____
2. _____
3. _____

What one thing will I do even better tomorrow?
_____

What was the most important lesson I learned today about today's key to unlocking my success?
_____
_____
_____

Personal Development

This evening I read 10 pages of: _____
Or I listened to 30 minutes of: _____

Affirmations (Write two new affirmations that you've discovered during the day)

I _____

I _____

My Why _____
_____

Day 17

Day 18

Morning

Today's Key: BE COMMITTED TO THE PROCESS

My Why: _____
_____

Daily Affirmations:

I _____

I _____

I _____

I _____

I _____

Personal Development

This morning I read 10 pages of: _____

Or I listened to 30 minutes of: _____

Five things I can do between today and this time tomorrow that will help me grow in today's key and become more successful.

1. _____
2. _____
3. _____
4. _____
5. _____

Two ways I can use today's key to sow into someone else's life and dreams today.

1. _____
2. _____

Evening

Daily Reflections

What three things did I do very well today? In what area was I most successful?

1 _____

2 _____

3 _____

What one thing will I do even better tomorrow?

_____

What was the most important lesson I learned today about today's key to unlocking my success?

_____

_____

_____

Personal Development

This evening I read 10 pages of: _____

Or I listened to 30 minutes of: _____

Affirmations (Write two new affirmations that you've discovered during the day)

I _____

I _____

My Why _____

_____

Day

18

Day 19

Morning

Today's Key: MAKE THE MOST OF EVERY DAY

My Why: _____

_____

Daily Affirmations:

I _____

I _____

I _____

I _____

I _____

Personal Development

This morning I read 10 pages of: _____

Or I listened to 30 minutes of: _____

Five things I can do between today and this time tomorrow that will help me grow in today's key and become more successful.

1. _____
2. _____
3. _____
4. _____
5. _____

Two ways I can use today's key to sow into someone else's life and dreams today.

1. _____
2. _____

Evening

Daily Reflections

What three things did I do very well today? In what area was I most successful?

1. _____
2. _____
3. _____

What one thing will I do even better tomorrow?

_____

What was the most important lesson I learned today about today's key to unlocking my success?

_____

_____

_____

Personal Development

This evening I read 10 pages of: _____
Or I listened to 30 minutes of: _____

Affirmations (Write two new affirmations that you've discovered during the day)

I _____

I _____

My Why _____

_____

Day 19

Day 20

Morning

Today's Key: DON'T EVER QUIT

My Why: _____
_____

Daily Affirmations:

I _____

I _____

I _____

I _____

I _____

Personal Development

This morning I read 10 pages of: _____

Or I listened to 30 minutes of: _____

Five things I can do between today and this time tomorrow that will help me grow in today's key and become more successful.

1. _____
2. _____
3. _____
4. _____
5. _____

Two ways I can use today's key to sow into someone else's life and dreams today.

1. _____
2. _____

Evening

Daily Reflections

What three things did I do very well today? In what area was I most successful?
1. _____
2. _____
3. _____

What one thing will I do even better tomorrow?
_____

What was the most important lesson I learned today about today's key to unlocking my success?
_____
_____
_____

Personal Development

This evening I read 10 pages of: _____
Or I listened to 30 minutes of: _____

Affirmations *(Write two new affirmations that you've discovered during the day)*

I _____

I _____

My Why _____
_____

Day

20

Day 21

Morning

Today's Key: THE GAME PLAN

My Why: _____
_____

Daily Affirmations:

I _____

I _____

I _____

I _____

I _____

Personal Development

This morning I read 10 pages of: _____

Or I listened to 30 minutes of: _____

Five things I can do between today and this time tomorrow that will help me grow in today's key and become more successful.

1. _____
2. _____
3. _____
4. _____
5. _____

Two ways I can use today's key to sow into someone else's life and dreams today.

1. _____
2. _____

Evening

Daily Reflections

What three things did I do very well today? In what area was I most successful?
1. _____
2. _____
3. _____

What one thing will I do even better tomorrow?
_____

What was the most important lesson I learned today about today's key to unlocking my success?
_____
_____
_____

Personal Development

This evening I read 10 pages of: _____
Or I listened to 30 minutes of: _____

Affirmations (Write two new affirmations that you've discovered during the day)

I _____

I _____

My Why _____
_____

Day 21

Success Is In My Hand

Congratulations! If you've completed this workbook in 21 days then you should now be in the habit of daily affirmations and personal development, looking at your Why everyday and using it to motivate you and setting goals daily and reflecting on them nightly. You've read the book and completed the workbook but you've just started your journey to your destiny.

Unlocking the successful you is a life-long process but you have done what it takes to get the keys to the lock. You have been educated, empowered and equipped to be successful. God has designed you for a great purpose and expects you to walk in your destiny. The chains of mediocrity have been broken off of your life and most importantly they've been broken off of your mind. Your stumbling blocks are now your stepping-stones and your dreams are now becoming reality.

Your final task is to "Pay it Forward". Decide whose life you're going to help change by exposing them to the same information you were exposed to. No great accomplishment was ever achieved by just one person. The more people you help become successful, the more successful you'll become. Write down the names of the first three people to whom you're going to recommend this book.

1. _____
2. _____
3. _____

In this final space write down what you have learned about yourself, where you see yourself in the next five to ten years and any final thoughts about your process of Unlocking the Successful Person God Designed You To Be.

_____
_____
_____
_____
_____
_____
_____

Dear Friend,

Congratulations for completing your 21-Day Course. Success is truly in your hands.

I feel confident that after reading the readings, saying your daily affirmations, doing your daily personal development, looking at your Why everyday and reflecting on each day, that you have grown tremendously and are well on your way to unlocking the successful person God designed you to be.

I am anxious to here what impact these 21 days has had on your life. Please send me an email of your story to stories@ryancgreene.com. Your story may be featured in an upcoming newsletter, article, or book. You never know who else is *going* through and needs to here how you *made* it through. May God continue to bless you and all of your endeavors.

I look forward to meeting you sometime in the future. Stay posted to www.ryancgreene.com to see when I'll be in your city.

Success Is In Your Hand,

Ryan C. Greene

About **Ryan C. Greene**

- ✓ Life-Changing Author
- ✓ Radio Talk-Show Host
- ✓ Renowned Speaker
- ✓ Successful Entrepreneur
- ✓ Seminar Leader & Trainer
- ✓ Business Consultant

Ryan C. Greene's leadership development began at a very young age. His single mother, Jacqueline, raised Ryan with his younger sister Stacie in the suburbs of Baltimore, MD. Ryan became the man of the house quickly as a "latch-key kid" at the age of eight. He attributes his determination, commitment to succeed and never give up attitude to watching his mother sacrifice her life for the life of her kids. Watching his mother fight to make ends meet, support her family and fight through her sickle cell anemia, gave Ryan the determined resolve to be the one to make a difference in his family.

Ryan is making that difference today, as he is quickly becoming one of the most sought after speakers and trainers on the East Coast. In January 2005, Ryan founded Bakari Book Publishers and self published his first book, *Success Is In Your Hand: 19 Keys To Unlocking The Successful Person You Were Designed To Be*. Ryan's next book *My Little Black Book Of Leadership: 15 Business Leadership Lessons I Learned From My Ex-Girlfriends*, will be released in the Winter of 2008. In January 2006, Ryan became the Executive Producer and Host of his own weekly radio talk show, *The Ryan C Greene Show*. Through the publishing company and radio show Ryan hopes to change as many lives as possible by delivering high-impact relevant solutions for unlocking one's full potential and realizing their individual destiny.

Ryan graduated from Hampton University in Hampton, VA in 1997 with a Bachelors of Science Degree in Marketing and is currently attaining a Masters Degree in Organizational Leadership with a concentration in Sales Management from Regent University in Virginia Beach, VA. After several years of job hopping and realizing that his place was not in Corporate America, Ryan sought to start his own business. Realizing that God had blessed him with the love of public speaking and a passion to see others achieve more and reach their full potential, Ryan was inspired to start a Personal Development Company. In 2003, Ryan founded Maximum Leadership Concepts. Maximum Leadership Concepts' mission is to Educate, Empower, and Equip Today's Leaders. This is accomplished through powerful keynote speeches, life-changing interactive seminars, focused corporate and organizational trainings, easy to read and apply books and other resources aimed toward adults, young-adults, professional and church leaders and aspiring business owners. Maximum Leadership Concepts is based in Baltimore, MD and also provides one on one business consultation.

Ryan speaks from the heart and his genuine, informative, and humorous presentations have already changed countless lives. He has been featured in a wide array of print, radio and television media. He is a contributing writer for Channel Magazine, Vision Magazine and Briefcase Magazine, has co-hosted "Briefcase Radio" on WEAA 88.9FM Baltimore and hosted "In Good Company" television talk show on Morgan State TV. Ryan has also founded The Jacqueline M Kidd Foundation, a non-profit foundation named after his mother that donates money to sickle cell research and awards college scholarships.

Ryan resides in Baltimore, MD with his wife Leslie and two children, Jordan and Jayden.

Be sure to take advantage of all of the
Success Is In Your Hand **Resources**
And begin unlocking the successful person you were designed to be today!

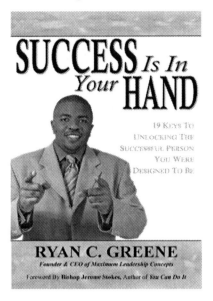

Success Is In Your Hand **Paperback Book**

Success Is In Your Hand **e-Book (PDF file)**

Success Is In Your Hand **Book-On-CD**

These and other great success and personal development

Resources from Ryan C. Greene

are available at

www.RyanCGreene.com

Get Personal Success Training By Enrolling in The Success Academy

When you enroll in The Success Academy you will:

- Receive Over 31 hours of personal consultation and mentoring from myself
- Online access to Download Audio Recordings of each 90 minute class
- Receive an Autographed copy of my book Success Is In Your Hand
- The "Million Dollar Success Library" of my Favorite Personal Development Books
- Get a FREE Bonus CD to launch your personal development efforts
- Engage in Intensive Learning of my 19 Keys to Unlocking Your Success
- Walk through a Daily Game Plan to find your purpose and maximize your success
- Get Life Changing Training from other experts in my Success Circle
- Discover how to go full throttle after your purpose and destiny
- Interact with like-minded people pushing on their journey to successful living
- Share your dreams and get expert advice to help make them come true
- Receive discounts on other Maximum Leadership Concepts events

Sign up today at www.ryancgreene.com

THE RYAN C. GREENE Show

The Ryan C. Greene Show was developed by Ryan C. Greene with the sole purpose of Educating, Empowering and Equipping listeners with the tools necessary to unlock the successful person they were designed to be so they may walk in their full destiny and purpose.

This interactive radio show, which reaches 7.5 Million people, not only gives the listeners a half-hour of life changing substance from knowledgeable guests, but it will keep listeners eagerly and anxiously anticipating the next week's show. **The Ryan C. Greene Show** focuses on Entrepreneurship, Leadership, and Success in Business, Life and Health.

Monthly Programming Series Include:

Every 1st Sunday: "The Business Of..." Series
This series explores the business side of selected industries in an effort to shed light on business opportunities and show ways to grow and improve existing businesses

Every Last Sunday: "Leadership University" Series
At the end of every month, school is in session as a leadership quality or issue is discussed with some of the most renowned leaders and teachers on leadership.

Each show is also full of Weekly Features designed to give listeners more keys to unlocking their success. Personal Development is encouraged through the **"Book of the Month"** and every show ends with a call to action in the **"Motivational Minute"**.

Ryan C. Greene is an Author, Motivational Speaker, Entrepreneur, Business Consultant and Executive Producer & Host of his own Weekly Radio Talk Show. He is the CEO and Founder of a personal development company, Maximum Leadership Concepts and a book publishing company, Bakari Book Publishers.

Ryan is the author of *Success Is In Your Hand: Unlocking The Successful Person You Were Designed To Be* and he is quickly becoming one of the most sought after speakers on the East Coast. He has been featured in a wide array of print, radio and television media. He is a staff writer for *Channel Magazine* and has also written for *The Network Marketing Magazine*, *Vision Magazine* and *Briefcase Magazine*. Ryan co-hosts "Briefcase Radio" on WEAA 88.9FM Baltimore and is the stand-in host of "In Good Company", a television talk show on entrepreneurship for Morgan State TV.

Ryan graduated from Hampton University in Hampton, VA with a B.S. in Marketing and he currently resides in Baltimore, MD.

LIVE SHOW TIME
LIVE Every Sunday 4pm–4:30pm EST (24hr Replay Available)
www.blogtalkradio.com/theryancgreeneshow
Call In # 646-652-2647

www.blogtalkradio.com/ theryancgreeneshow

EDUCATE, EMPOWER, AND EQUIP TODAY'S LEADERS

Ryan C. Greene